Collection « Lire en anglais »
dirigée par Henri Yvinec

English Ghost Stories

Choix et annotations par Marielle Law
et John S. Law

LE LIVRE DE POCHE

La collection "Les Langues Modernes" n'a pas de lien avec l'A.P.L.V. et les ouvrages qu'elle publie le sont sous sa seule responsabilité.

© Librairie Générale Française, 1992, pour la présentation et les notes.
ISBN : 978-2-253-05599-0 – 1re publication LGF

Sommaire

Introduction 7

The Ghost Story 9

Catherine Wells : *The Ghost* 13

H. R. Wakefield : *Nurse's Tale* 29

Richard Hughes : *The Ghost* 51

Elizabeth Walter : *Dual Control* 63

Alfred Noyes : *Midnight Express* 91

Vocabulary 107

Abbreviations

sb.: somebody
sth.: something
fam.: familiar
sl.: slang (argotique)

Tout naturellement, après quelques années d'étude d'une langue étrangère, naît l'envie de lire dans le texte. Mais, par ailleurs, le vocabulaire dont on dispose est souvent insuffisant. La perspective de recherches lexicales multipliées chez le lecteur isolé, la présentation fastidieuse du vocabulaire, pour le professeur, sont autant d'obstacles redoutables. C'est pour tenter de les aplanir que nous proposons cette nouvelle collection.

Celle-ci constitue une étape vers la lecture autonome, sans dictionnaire ni traduction, grâce à des notes facilement repérables. S'agissant des élèves de lycée, les ouvrages de cette collection seront un précieux instrument pédagogique pour les enseignants en langues étrangères puisque les recommandations pédagogiques officielles (Bulletin officiel de l'Éducation nationale du 9 juillet 1987 et du 9 juin 1988) les invitent à "faire de l'entraînement à la lecture individuelle une activité régulière" qui pourra aller jusqu'à une heure hebdomadaire. Ces recueils de textes devraient ainsi servir de complément à l'étude de la civilisation. Celle-ci sera également abordée dans des volumes consacrés aux presses étrangères.

Le lecteur trouvera donc :

En page de gauche

Des textes contemporains — nouvelles ou courts romans — choisis pour leur intérêt littéraire et la qualité de leur langue.

En page de droite

Des notes juxtalinéaires rédigées dans la langue du texte, qui aident le lecteur à

Comprendre

Tous les mots et expressions difficiles contenus dans la ligne de gauche sont reproduits en caractères gras et expliqués dans le contexte.

Observer

Des notes d'observation de la langue soulignent le caractère idiomatique de certaines tournures ou constructions.

Apprendre

Dans un but d'enrichissement lexical, certaines notes proposent enfin des synonymes, des antonymes, des expressions faisant appel aux mots qui figurent dans le texte.

Grammaire

Le lecteur trouvera, au moins pour les nouvelles courtes et sous des formes diverses selon les volumes, un rappel des structures rebelles les plus courantes — c'est-à-dire des tournures les plus difficilement assimilées par les francophones. Des chiffres de référence renverront au contexte et aux explications données dans les *Grammaires actives* (de l'anglais, de l'allemand, de l'espagnol, du portugais...) publiées au *Livre de Poche*.

Vocabulaire

En fin de volume une liste de plus de 1 500 mots contenus dans les textes, suivis de leur traduction, comporte, entre autres, les verbes irréguliers et les mots qui n'ont pas été annotés faute de place ou parce que leur sens était évident dans le contexte. Grâce à ce lexique on pourra, en dernier recours, procéder à quelques vérifications ou faire un bilan des mots retenus au cours des lectures.

Henri YVINEC

The Ghost Story

"I don't believe in ghosts, but I'm afraid of them."
Madame du Deffand, quoted by Kingsley Amis.

If you ask people what they expect from ghost stories, most will answer that they expect to be frightened. In other words, to be worthy of its name, a ghost story, like the ghost it features, must always haunt those who encounter it.

This haunting feeling is basically a sort of uneasiness, a blend of fear and mystery which is not however to be confused with what we experience from either horror stories or detective novels. The imagination is blocked by horror and the sense of fear and mystery aroused by crime fiction is always dispelled at the end. In the ghost story, on the other hand, the imagination expands for it is confronted not with a monster or a murderer but with a supernatural being, whose mysterious presence always lingers on in our minds beyond the final pages.

This haunting quality has been our main guide in selecting the stories for this book. To achieve it, they have let the supernatural intrude as discreetly and as convincingly as possible upon what we call "everyday reality". Banishing the conventional spooks of folklore and Gothic fantasy, they have concentrated instead on building up a special kind of atmosphere in which the senses of the main character are often stimulated by his or her being isolated in a lonely bedroom, or office building. Only in this carefully constructed atmosphere can the character's imagination, and the reader's too, expand in terror until both become aware of the tangible presence of the intangible, which is what the experience of being haunted really involves.

The need to convey this experience does not mean that ghost stories lack variety. Not only may the haunting experience itself range in intensity from the pleasant to the terrifying, ghosts also allow for considerable characterisation as they are (or were !) human beings, endowed with the full gamut of human emotions, from ardent love to vengeful hatred. What is more, they can function as catalysts for the exacerbated emotions of other characters (*Dual Control*), or as metaphors for a character's state of mind (Richard Hughes's *The Ghost*). In short, there is a great deal of diversity possible within what might seem, at first sight, to be a very limited genre.

This genre belongs to the literature of the fantastic, which, as far as the English tradition is concerned, has its roots in the Gothic novels of the late eighteenth century, especially Horace Walpole's *The Castle of Otranto* (1764). Of course, ghosts had already figured in many works of English literature including Shakespeare's *Hamlet* and *Macbeth*, but they were not the central interest that they must be for such works to qualify as ghost stories.

The first ghost story as such was no doubt Walter Scott's *Wandering Willie's Tale* (1824). A decade later came the work of the first writer to specialise in the genre and one of its undoubted masters, J. Sheridan Le Fanu, whose stories were published in magazine form, establishing a tradition that Charles Dickens was to encourage with his own magazines and contributions such as *The Signalman*. Ghost stories were to become increasingly popular in the latter half of the nineteenth century no doubt in part because of the Victorian interest in spiritualism. Women writers like Mrs Gaskell and Mrs Oliphant contributed some of the finest as did such famous authors as Rudyard Kipling, Robert Louis Stevenson, and Thomas Hardy.

The early decades of the present century witnessed the emergence of several specialists — Cynthia Asquith, Algernon Blackwood, A. M. Burrage, Walter de la Mare, Lord Dunsany, E. F. Benson, H. R. Wakefield, and, notably, M. R. James, whom many consider to be the master of the genre. At the same time, the ghost story continued to attract many famous names like H. G. Wells and Somerset Maugham. If it has lost a little of its popularity in the latter half of this century, the quality of the stories produced, whether by the specialists like Elizabeth Walter and Rosemary Timperley or by distinguished contributors like Elizabeth Bowen or L. P. Hartley, has in no way diminished.

Examples from most of these authors can be found in two representative anthologies in Penguin: *Roald Dahl's Book of Ghost Stories* and *The Penguin Book of Ghost Stories (ed. J. A. Cuddon)*, as well as in *The Penguin Complete Ghost Stories of M. R. James*. Hardback anthologies include *The Oxford Book of Ghost Stories* and *The Virago Book of Ghost Stories*, whose contributors are all women, illustrating their particular talent for the genre. Finally, two stories have already been published in the *Lire en anglais* series: *A Night at a Cottage* by Richard Hughes in *Thirteen Modern English and American Short Stories* and Somerset Maugham's *The Taipan* in *The Escape and Other Short Stories*.

The Ghost

by Catherine Wells (1872-1927)

Amy Catherine Robbins was an artist and writer who in 1895 married H. G. Wells, the author of *The Time Machine* and *The War of the Worlds*, as well as of several memorable ghost stories. On her death, her husband collected twenty-one of her poems and stories in *The Book of Catherine Wells* (1928). In his preface, Wells speaks of "that predisposition towards a haunting dreamland fantasy of fear", which he considered to be characteristic of her work, and of which the following story is a fine example.

The way the author recreates the atmosphere of the lonely room and builds up tension as the girl waits for her visitor to reappear makes this apparently simple ghost story marvellously suspenseful.

She was a girl of fourteen, and she sat propped up with pillows in an old four-poster bed, coughing a little with the feverish cold that kept her there. She was tired of reading by lamplight, and she lay and listened to the few sounds that she could hear, and looked into the fire. From downstairs, down the wide, rather dark, oak-panelled corridor hung with brown ochre pictures of tremendous naval engagements exploding fierily in their centres, down the broad stone stairs that ended in a
10 heavy, creaking, nail-studded door, there blew in to her remoteness sometimes a gust of dance music. Cousins and cousins and cousins were down there, and Uncle Timothy, as host, leading the fun. Several of them had danced into her room during the day, and said that her illness was a "perfect shame", told her that the skating in the park was "too heavenly", and danced out again. Uncle Timothy had been as kind as kind could be. But—Downstairs all the full cup of happiness the lonely child had looked forward to so eagerly for a month, was
20 running away like liquid gold.

She watched the flames of the big wood fire in the open grate flicker and fall. She had sometimes to clench her hands to prevent herself from crying. She had discovered—so early was she beginning to collect her little stock of feminine lore—that if you swallowed hard and rapidly as the tears gathered, that you could prevent your eyes brimming over. She wished someone would come. There was a bell within her reach, but she could think of no plausible excuse for ringing it. She wished
30 there was more light in the room. The big fire lit up cheerfully when the logs flared high; but when they only glowed, the dark shadows crept down from the

propped up: with her back on a support

pillow(s): cushion □ **4-poster:** = 4-pillar □ **coughing:** smoke makes you cough □ **feverish cold:** febrile illness □ **tired of:** no more interested in

few: not many □ **fire:** flames making the room hot

wide: spacious □ **rather:** a little □ **dark:** ≠ bright □ **oak-panelled:** with panels of wood; **oak** = *chêne* □ **hung:** decorated

tremendous: impressive □ **fierily:** with lots of flames

broad: wide □ **stone:** *pierre* □ **stairs:** to go up or down in a house □ **heavy:** ≠ light □ **nail-studded:** *clouté* □ **there...gust of dance music:** music was carried to her isolated bedroom on the air like a wind every time the door opened

leading the fun: organising the amusements □ **several:** a small number

shame: = pity: they were very sorry she was ill □ **skating:** *patinage* □ **heavenly:** divine

as kind...could be: as compassionate as possible

full: filled completely □ **lonely:** with no company

looked forward to...eagerly: waited for...impatiently

running away: disappearing □ **gold:** precious yellow metal

grate: metal bars holding wood □ **flicker:** tremble □ **clench:** close firmly □ **prevent...crying:** stop water falling from her eyes

early: near the beginning of her life

feminine lore: information about women □ **swallowed hard:** absorbed her saliva vigorously □ **tears gathered:** water came into her eyes □ **brimming over:** letting water fall

bell: instrument whose sound attracts attention □ **within...reach:** which her hand could touch □ **ringing:** making the bell give its sound □ **lit up...:** gave a pleasant light

logs flared...glowed: wood burned with flames, then without

shadows crept: dark forms moved

ceiling and gathered in the corners against the panelling. She turned from the scrutiny of the room to the bright circle of light under the lamp on the table beside her, and the companionable suggestiveness of the currant jelly and spoon, grapes and lemonade and little pile of books and kindly fuss that shone warmly and comfortingly there. Perhaps it would not be long before Mrs Bunting, her uncle's housekeeper, would come in again and sit down and talk to her.

10   Mrs Bunting, very probably, was more occupied than usual that evening. There were several extra guests, another house-party had motored over for the evening, and they had brought with them a romantic figure, a celebrity, no less a personage than the actor Percival East. The girl had indeed broken down from her fortitude that afternoon when Uncle Timothy had told her of this visitor. Uncle Timothy was surprised; it was only another schoolgirl who would have understood fully what it meant to be denied by a mere cold the
20 chance of meeting face to face that chivalrous hero of drama; another girl who had glowed at his daring, wept at his noble renunciations, been made happy, albeit enviously and vicariously, by his final embrace with the lady of his love.

    "There, there, dear child," Uncle Timothy had said, patting her shoulder and greatly distressed. "Never mind, never mind. If you can't get up I'll bring him in to see you here. I promise I will... But the *pull* these chaps have over you little women," he went on, half to
30 himself....

    The panelling creaked. Of course, it always did in these old houses. She was of that order of apprehensive,

ceiling: top of room □ **gathered:** converged □ **corner(s):** angle □ **panelling:** panels of wood on walls □ **turned...scrutiny:** stopped her examination

companionable suggestiveness: friendly associations □ **currant:** red fruit □ **spoon:** to take soup with □ **grape(s):** wine comes from grapes □ **kindly fuss:** signs of affection and care

comfortingly: consolingly, reassuringly

housekeeper: one who organizes the work in a house that is not her property

usual: normally □ **extra:** supplementary □ **guests:** people invited

house-party...motored over: group of guests at another house in the country, who had arrived by car

no less...than the actor: in fact the famous actor

indeed: in fact □ **broken down from:** abandoned

fortitude: courage

fully: entirely □ **meant:** signified □ **denied:** refused □ **mere:** simple; he is a mere child = he is just a child

glowed: felt hot with emotion □ **daring:** audacity □ **wept:** cried; water came to her eyes with emotion □ **albeit:** even if

vicariously: through the actress's experience □ **embrace:** act of taking sb. into your arms

there, there: expression to console someone who is crying

patting: tapping □ **shoulder:** where arm joins body □ **greatly:** very □ **never mind:** it is not important

pull: fascination

chap(s): (fam.) man □ **went on:** continued □ **half to himself:** partly speaking to himself

creaked: made a sound; wood creaks as temperature changes

order: sort, kind, type

slightly nervous people who do not believe in ghosts, but all the same hope devoutly they may never see one. Surely it was a long time since any one had visited her; it would be hours, she supposed, before the girl who had the room next her own, into which a communicating door comfortingly led, came up to bed. If she rang, it took a minute or two before any one reached her from the remote servants' quarters. There ought soon, she thought, to be a housemaid about the corridor outside,
10 tidying up the bedrooms, putting coal on the fires, and making suchlike companionable noises. That would be pleasant. How bored one got in bed anyhow, and how dreadful it was, how unbearably dreadful it was that she should be stuck in bed now, missing everything, missing every bit of the glorious glowing time that was slipping away down there. At that she had to begin swallowing her tears again.

With a sudden burst of sound, a storm of clapping and laughter, the heavy door at the foot of the big stairs
20 swung open and closed. Footsteps came upstairs, and she heard men's voices approaching. Uncle Timothy. He knocked at the door ajar. "Come in," she cried gladly. With him was a quiet-faced greyish-haired man of middle age. Then uncle had sent for the doctor after all!

"Here is another of your worshippers, Mr East," said Uncle Timothy.

Mr East! She realised in a flash that she had expected him in purple brocade, powdered hair, and ruffles of
30 fine lace. Her uncle smiled at her disconcerted face.

"She doesn't seem to recognise you, Mr East," said Uncle Timothy.

slightly: a little □ **believe in ghosts:** consider ghosts to be real
hope: wish □ **devoutly:** sincerely

next: very near, just beside □ **her own:** her personal room
comfortingly led: reassuringly opened into □ **it took...:** a
minute...was necessary □ **reached:** came to
remote: distant □ **ought soon:** will probably (be) in a short time
housemaid: female servant □ (moving) **about** (in)
tidying up: arranging □ **coal:** black substance
suchlike: similar □ **companionable noises:** friendly sounds
bored: ≠ interested □ **got:** became □ **anyhow:** in any case
unbearably: unendurably □ **dreadful:** terrible
stuck: immobilised □ **missing:** being absent from
bit: part □ **glowing:** radiant □ **slipping away:** passing inexorably
at that: at that thought

burst: explosion □ **storm:** clamour □ **clapping:** applause
laughter: sounds of amusement □ **foot:** base
swung open: opened suddenly □ **footsteps:** sound of walking

knocked: tapped □ **ajar:** open a little □ **gladly:** happily
quiet: calm □ **greyish:** a little grey, not black nor white
middle age: not young, not old □ **sent for:** asked to come

worshipper(s): fervent admirer

in a flash: instantly □ **expected:** imagined
brocade: *brocart* □ **ruffles:** *jabot et manchettes*
lace: *dentelle* □ **smiled:** had an amused expression on his face
recognise you: know who you are

"Of course I do," she declared bravely, and sat up, flushed with excitement and her feverishness, bright-eyed and with ruffled hair. Indeed she began to see the stage hero she remembered and the kindly-faced man before her flow together like a composite portrait. There was the little nod of the head, there was the chin, yes! and the eyes, now she came to look at them. "Why were they all clapping you?" she asked.

"Because I had just promised to frighten them out of
10 their wits," replied Mr East.

"Oh, how?"

"Mr East," said Uncle Timothy, "is going to dress up as our long-lost ghost, and give us a really shuddering time of it downstairs."

"*Are* you?" cried the girl with all the fierce desire that only a girl can utter in her voice. "Oh, why am I ill like this, Uncle Timothy? I'm not ill really. Can't you see I'm better? I've been in bed all day. I'm perfectly well. Can't I come down, Uncle *dear*—can't I?"

20 In her excitement she was half out of bed. "There, there, child," soothed Uncle Timothy, hastily smoothing the bedclothes and trying to tuck her in.

"But *can't* I?"

"Of course, if you want to be thoroughly frightened, frightened out of your wits, mind you," began Percival East.

"I do, I *do*," she cried, bouncing up and down in her bed.

"I'll come and show myself when I'm dressed up,
30 before I go down."

"Oh please, please," she cried back radiantly. A private performance all to herself! "Will you be perfectly

of course: naturally □ **bravely:** courageously
flushed: hot and red in the face □ **feverishness:** febrile state
ruffled: disarranged □ **stage:** platform where actors stand
remembered: reviewed in her mind □ **kindly:** benevolent
flow...portrait: converge to form one image
nod: movement □ **chin:** part of face under mouth
came to: began to
clapping: applauding
frighten...wits: terrify them so much that they will lose their
reason (wits) □ **replied:** answered

dress up: disguise himself
long-lost: that disappeared a long time ago □ **shuddering...it:**
experience that will make us shudder (tremble) with terror
fierce: intense
utter: express □ **ill:** unwell, a sick girl

dear: cherished; affectionate address: my dear (uncle)

soothed: consoled □ **hastily:** quickly □ **smoothing:** arranging
bedclothes: what covered her in bed □ **tuck her in:** fix the
bedclothes firmly around her
thoroughly: completely
mind you: consider attentively what I am saying

bouncing up and down: moving in an agitated way while sitting

show: present

radiantly: joyously
performance: show □ **all to herself:** just for her

awful?" she laughed exultantly.

"As ever I can," smiled Mr East, and turned to follow Uncle Timothy out of the room. "You know," he said, holding the door and looking back at her with mock seriousness, "I shall look rather horrid, I expect. Are you sure you won't mind?"

"Mind—when it's you?" laughed the girl.

He went out of the room, shutting the door.

"Rum-ti-tum, ti-tum, ti-ty," she hummed gaily, and
10 wriggled down into her bedclothes again, straightened the sheet over her chest, and prepared to wait.

She lay quietly for some time, with a smile on her face, thinking of Percival East and fitting his grave, kindly face back into its various dramatic settings. She was quite satisfied with him. She began to go over in her mind in detail the last play in which she had seen him act. How splendid he had looked when he fought the duel! She couldn't imagine him gruesome, she thought. What would he do with himself?

20 Whatever he did, she wasn't going to be frightened. He shouldn't be able to boast he had frightened *her*. Uncle Timothy would be there too, she supposed. Would he?

Footsteps went past her door outside, along the corridor, and died away. The big door at the end of the stairs opened and clanged shut.

Uncle Timothy had gone down.

She waited on.

A log, burnt through the middle to a ruddy thread,
30 fell suddenly in two tumbling pieces on the hearth. She started at the sound. How quiet everything was. How much longer would he be, she wondered. The fire

awful: terrifying ☐ **exultantly:** enthusiastically
as ever I can: as awful as possible ☐ **follow:** go after

mock: false, affected
look: appear ☐ **horrid:** horrible ☐ **expect:** suppose
mind: have objections; do you mind my looking horrid; I don't
mind (object to) your being horrid
shutting: closing
hummed: sang to herself without forming real words
wriggled down: descended like a serpent ☐ **straightened:**
arranged ☐ **sheet:** fine, white part of bedclothes ☐ **chest:** part
of body above abdomen
fitting...back into: re-associating with
setting(s): *décor*
quite: completely ☐ **go over:** review
play: drama; tragedy or comedy with actors
fought: participated in (to fight a battle, a campaign)
gruesome: hideous
what...himself?: how would he disguise himself?
whatever he did: he could do what he liked
boast: proclaim with arrogance
would be: perhaps he would be there, perhaps he would not

footsteps: sounds made by people walking
died away: were progressively inaudible
clanged shut: shut with an echoing metallic sound

waited on: continued to wait
log: piece of wood ☐ **middle:** centre ☐ **ruddy:** red ☐ **thread:** fine
piece ☐ **tumbling:** rolling ☐ **hearth:** place where fire burns
started: made a sudden movement in alarm
wondered: asked herself

wanted making up, the pieces of wood collecting
together. Should she ring? But he might come in just
when the servant was mending the fire, and that would
spoil his entry. The fire could wait....

The room was very still, and, with the fallen fire,
darker. She heard no more any sound at all from
downstairs. That was because her door was shut. All
day it had been open, but now the last slender link that
held her to downstairs was broken.

10   The lamp flame gave a sudden fitful leap. Why? Was
it going out? Was it?—no.

She hoped he wouldn't jump out at her, but of course
he wouldn't. Anyhow, whatever he did she wouldn't be
frightened—really frightened. Forewarned is forearmed.

Was that a sound? She started up, her eyes on the
door. Nothing.

But surely, the door had minutely moved, it did not
sit back quite so close into its frame! Perhaps it—She
20   was sure it had moved. Yes, it had moved—opened an
inch, and slowly, as she watched, she saw a thread of
light grow between the edge of the door and its frame,
grow almost imperceptibly wider, and stop.

He could never come through that? It must have
yawned open of its own accord. Her heart began to beat
rather quickly. She could see only the upper part of the
door, the foot of her bed hid the lower third....

Her attention tightened. Suddenly, as suddenly as a
pistol shot, she saw that there was a little figure like a
30   dwarf near the wall, between the door and the fireplace.
It was a little cloaked figure, no higher than the table.
How *did* he do it? It was moving slowly, very slowly,

wanted making up: needed more wood □ **collecting:** = wanted collecting = needed collecting / to be collected
mending: reconstructing
spoil his entry: ruin the dramatic effect when he came in
still: silent
no...at all: not one sound

slender: tenuous, fragile □ **link:** connection, tie, bond
broken: interrupted
fitful: irregular □ **leap:** jump
going out: going to disappear
jump out at: surge up in front of
anyhow: in any case
forewarned is forearmed: (proverb) if you know what is going to take place, you are prepared to accept it
started up: sat up in alarm

minutely: only a very little (minute = microscopic) □ **did not sit back...frame:** was not completely shut

inch: 2.54 cm. □ **thread:** little ray
edge: extremity □ **frame:** part of wall where door is fixed
wider: more open
come through: traverse
yawned...accord: opened like a mouth by itself □ **heart:** pump of body □ **upper part:** top, summit
hid: made invisible □ **lower:** ≠ upper □ **third:** one of three equal parts □ **tightened:** intensified
shot: explosive sound □ **figure:** silhouette
dwarf: very small man (Snow White and the Seven Dwarfs)
cloaked: wearing a cloak (cloak = long cape)

towards the fire, as if it was quite unconscious of her; it
was wrapped about in a cloak that trailed, with a
slouched hat on its head bent down to its shoulders. She
gripped the clothes with her hands, it was so queer, so
unexpected; she gave a little gasping laugh to break the
tension of the silence—to show she appreciated him.

The dwarf stopped dead at the sound, and turned its
face round to her.

Oh! but she was frightened! it was a dead white face,
10 a long pointed face hunched between its shoulders, there
was no colour in the eyes that stared at her! How did he
do it, how *did* he do it? It was too good. She laughed
again nervously, and with a clutch of terror that she
could not control she saw the creature move out of the
shadow and come towards her. She braced herself with
all her might, she mustn't be frightened by a bit of
acting—he was coming nearer, it was horrible, horrible—right up to her bed. . . .

She flung her head beneath the bedclothes. Whether
20 she screamed or not she never knew. . . .

Some one was rapping at her door, speaking cheerily.
She took her head out of the clothes with a revulsion of
shame at her fright. The horrible little creature was
gone! Mr East was speaking at her door. What was it he
was saying? *What?*

"I'm ready now," he said. *"Shall I come in, and
begin?"*

towards: in the direction of
wrapped about: enveloped □ **trailed:** touched the floor
slouched hat: sort of sombrero □ **bent down:** inclined
gripped: seized □ **clothes:** bedclothes □ **queer:** bizarre
unexpected: surprising □ **gave...gasping laugh:** inhaled air when
laughing
dead: completely

dead white: as white as a dead man's face
hunched...shoulders: joined directly to shoulders
stared: looked fixedly

clutch: attack

shadow: obscurity □ **braced herself:** prepared herself for the
shock □ **might:** concentration □ **a bit of acting:** Mr East's
performance
right up to: very near
flung: pushed □ **beneath:** under □ **whether:** if
screamed: cried out in terror
rapping: knocking, tapping □ **cheerily:** in a friendly voice
revulsion: reaction
shame: embarrassment □ **fright:** terror □ **was gone:** had
disappeared

I'm ready: I've prepared my show

Grammaire au fil des nouvelles

En traduisant les phrases suivantes qui contiennent des difficultés grammaticales suggérées par les italiques, essayez de retrouver le texte anglais dont la page est indiquée par le premier chiffre et les lignes par les suivants ; les chiffres en gras renvoient à la Grammaire active *de l'anglais publiée au Livre de Poche.*

Elle *en avait assez de lire* (34. 3 - 4. p. 148).

Plusieurs d'*entre eux étaient entrés* dans sa chambre *en dansant* (34. 13.14. **p. 158**).

*L'*Oncle Timothy avait été *aussi* gentil *que* possible (34. 17. **pp. 72, 114**).

Elle regardait *trembler* les flammes (34. 21-22. **p. 60**).

Elle *aurait voulu* que quelqu'un *vienne* (34. 27-28. **p. 42**).

Madame Bunting était *plus* préoccupée *que d'habitude* (36. 10 - 11. **p. 114**).

Cela faisait longtemps que personne ne lui avait rendu visite (38. 3. **p. 34**).

Il *devrait* y avoir bientôt une bonne dans le couloir (38. 8 - 9. **p. 24**).

C'était *vraiment* épouvantable qu'elle *soit* clouée au lit (38. 13 - 14. **p. 146**).

Elle entendait des voix d'hommes *se rapprocher* (38. 21. **p. 60**).

Il y avait avec lui un homme *aux cheveux grisonnants et au visage serein* (38. 23. **p. 112**).

« Elle n'a pas l'air de vous reconnaître »... « *Bien sûr que si !* » déclara-t-elle (38. 31 - 40. 1. **p. 48**).

Je viendrai me montrer quand je *serai déguisé* (40. 29. **p. 38**).

Comme tout était silencieux ! (42. 31. **p. 146**).

Il *entrerait peut-être* juste au moment où la servante *serait en train de* ranimer le feu (44. 2-3. **pp. 22, 42**).

Quoi qu'il fît, elle ne *serait* pas effrayée (44. 13 - 14. **pp. 165, 42**).

Elle *avait dû* s'ouvrir toute seule (44. 24 - 25. **p. 26**).

Nurse's Tale

by H. R. Wakefield (1888-1964)

Herbert Russell Wakefield was born near Folkestone in Kent in 1888, the son of the Bishop of Birmingham. He was educated at Oxford University where he took a degree in Modern History. He worked as a private secretary, then as a publisher and journalist. Although only part of his work has been recently re-published, he is considered to be a major representative of the ghost story tradition in England. His first book of ghost stories, *They Return at Evening*, was published in 1928, to be followed by *Old Man's Beard* (1929), *Imagine a Man in a Box* (1931), and *The Clock strikes Twelve* (1940).

Many young children first heard about ghosts in a tale told to them by their nurses, and *Nurse's Tale* uses this familiar situation to counterbalance the suspense and terror present in this classic story of possession and vengeance, written by a man for whom ghosts were "never farther away than just round the corner from what is called *Reality*".

"Thanks awfully, Nurse; it's just what I wanted. But now I'm ten you've got to tell me about that kid Layton. You promised you would."

"I don't believe I ever promised."

"Yes, you did, you old fiend."

"You mustn't use such expressions, Master Gilbert, they're rude! You're too old for your age, that's what you are! And you read too many of those ghost books. That James, he gives me the creeps!"

10   "Oh, I love them, Nurse; especially, *Oh, whistle and I'll come to you*!"

That one about the bedclothes getting up and walking about, just when they'd made the bed, too? I can't see why people want to think of such things."

"Well I'm ten and you promised."

"And I hope you'll behave like ten; it's time you did. I dare say the other Marlborough boys will take you down a peg or two, when you get there."

"I shan't funk them. And shut up, Nurse, and shoot 20 the works!"

"Where ever did you learn that vulgar saying?"

"At the cinema. Oh, go on!"

"And give you dreams and get into trouble with your mamma. You're such a pest! Well, I'll tell you, but don't blame me if you can't sleep. Anyway, I know I shan't have any peace till I *do* tell you. Now, sit still and don't shuffle about.

"It's about twenty-five years since I first went to Layton Hall. Lady Layton died the night I arrived, poor 30 dear, and the funeral and the christening took place within a few days of each other. His Lordship was terribly sad. He was a fine gentleman, every inch a lord.

awfully: a lot □ **(child-)nurse:** woman paid to take care of a child □ **now** (that) □ **'ve got to:** must □ **kid:** (fam.) boy
you would (tell me)
believe: think
you...fiend: you old demon (note the emphatic use of "you")
Master: title of respect used by servant to address employer's children □ **rude:** impolite □ **old:** ≠ young

James: famous ghost-story writer □ **gives...creeps:** makes me tremble with terror, makes my flesh creep □ *Oh, whistle (sifflez) and I'll come to you:* James's most famous story
that one: that story □ **bedclothes:** covers on the bed
about: around the room
such things: things like that

I hope...ten: I'd like you to act like a ten-year-old boy
dare say: suppose □ **Marlborough** College is a famous school □
take you down a peg or two: make you more humble □ **get:** go
funk: be intimidated by □ **shut up:** be silent (rude) □ **shoot the works:** (sl.) tell me the story
ever: (emphatic) in the world □ **saying:** expression
go on!: please tell me!
and (if I do, I'll) **give** □ **(bad) dream(s):** vision □ **trouble:** difficulty □ **mamma:** elegant form of "mummy"
anyway: in any case □ **shan't:** shall not
peace: tranquillity □ **till:** until, before □ **still:** immobile
shuffle about: move your feet nervously
about: approximately
Hall: Manor □ **Lady:** Lord's wife □ **died:** stopped living
christening: baptism □ **took place:** were celebrated
within...other: almost in succession □ **His Lordship:** title for a lord □ **sad:** unhappy □ **every inch...:** a perfect lord

He was very tall, and handsome and quiet, and at first
he didn't seem to take to the baby—Jocelyn they named
him—but then afterwards he could hardly keep his
thoughts off him. At first I wondered why he seemed so
watchful and anxious, but one day the head gardener
told me there was a sort of mystery about the family.
The story was that a long while ago—hundreds of
years—they burnt a witch, at least I think she was a
witch—some bad lot, anyway—"

10   "But, Nurse, you don't believe in witches, do you?"

"I don't believe either way, but where I was brought
up plenty did. But, as I say, they burnt one of them, and
her small boy too. And it seems he was near his sixth
birthday, and this witch put a curse on the family—that
was the talk, anyway—saying that no Layton's eldest
son would live to be six. And they never had done after
that. So the place was always going to different parts of
the family. And that was why his Lordship was so
anxious about Master Jocelyn. He was a beautiful baby,
20 and very good—too good, I used to think. For he
hardly ever cried, not even when he was cutting his
teeth, and healthy babies ought to cry. You used to cry
till I could have choked you, you young limb, but then
you were never good. Now, don't pinch or I won't tell
you any more. Not that he was sickly, but he seemed to
be thinking his own thoughts all the while. But the first
time I found something really funny about him was
when he was about nine months old. At Layton there is
a long drive from the road to the Hall, twisting and
30 hilly, and about half-way up there was a dip in it—a
sort of valley. It was a lovely quiet spot, cut off from
everything, with fields on either side. It always used to

tall: ≠ small □ **handsome:** attractive □ **quiet:** calm
seem: appear □ **take to:** like, feel affection for
could hardly keep...him: thought about him almost all the time
wondered: asked myself
watchful: vigilant □ **head gardener:** principal gardener

while: time
witch: sorceress □ **at least:** I'm not sure but
lot: creature
believe in witches: think witches really exist
I...either way: I'm undecided □ **was brought up:** lived as a child
plenty did: many people believed
near: approaching
curse: malediction
talk: rumour □ **eldest:** first-born
done: lived to be six
place: manor

used to think: always thought □ **for:** because
hardly ever: practically never □ **he...teeth:** his first teeth were
growing □ **healthy...cry:** vigorous babies normally cry
choked: strangled □ **young limb:** young pest
pinch: use your fingers like pincers to make me suffer
sickly: delicate, in poor health
thinking...thoughts: preoccupied
funny: strange
twelve **months** in a year (note: a nine-month-old baby)
drive: private road □ **road:** public road □ **twisting:** sinuous
hilly: with ups and downs □ **half-way:** at equal distance □ **dip:**
depression □ **spot:** place □ **cut off:** isolated
field(s): area of grass □ **on either side:** right and left

give me the creeps a bit; I mean I wouldn't have walked along there alone after dark if I could have helped it."

"I wouldn't have minded. I bet I'd have gone!"

"Oh, you're very brave and full of swank in the morning with people about. But you weren't so brave in the cloisters at Norwich!"

"Well, something began to tap on the other side of the big door just as I reached it; and I thought it was beginning to open. And there wasn't anyone in the
10 Cathedral. Anyway, I was partly pretending."

"Did you put chalk on your face? That was white enough. Now, don't keep on interrupting. Well, as I said, it was just about Master Jocelyn's ninth month that I found he was queer about that bit of drive. As we got near it he'd waken and sit up in his pram and keep his eyes fixed on the field on the left side—coming down, that is. And he wouldn't lie down until we began to go up the hill on the other side, however much I tried to make him. And then the pucker left his little forehead
20 and he'd lie back and go to sleep again. As he got older he seemed to get more and more interested in that bit of the drive, and when he learned to walk he always insisted on getting out and going into the field, and almost the first thing he ever said after he'd learned to talk was, 'Pitty tees,' when he was out on the grass."

"But I thought you said it was just a field?"

"So it was. There was a tree or two, but they was on the other side of the drive."

"Then—"
30 "Now, Master Gilbert, don't keep on stopping me in the middle. I'm just telling you what happened. And what happened was that Master Jocelyn always behaved

a bit: a little □ **I mean:** that is to say
alone: ≠ in company □ **dark:** nightfall □ **helped it:** acted differently □ **minded:** had objections □ **I bet:** I'm sure
brave: courageous □ **swank:** arrogance
about: present
cloister(s): passageway round a garden in Norwich cathedral
side: part
as: when □ **reached it:** arrived there

partly: in part □ **pretending:** simulating
chalk: white substance teachers use to write on blackboards □
white enough: distinctly white □ **keep on:** persist in

was queer about: acted strangely concerning □ **bit:** part
'd waken: would frequently stop sleeping □ **pram:** vehicle for taking a baby for a walk
that is: to be more precise
however much I tried: resisting all my efforts
make him (go up) □ **pucker:** mark of anxiety □ **forehead:** between hair and nose □ **got:** became

almost: practically
pitty tees: baby talk for pretty (= attractive) trees; a cedar is a tree □ **field:** area of grass used as pasture
so it was: it was a field □ **they was:** they were (uneducated way of speaking)
then: (and what comes) after that?
now: expression used to stop sb. interrupting

behaved: acted

as if there was trees. It used to worry me—it wasn't natural—and I tried to get him past that dip, but he wouldn't let me, and then I tried keeping him in the garden, but he wouldn't let me do that either, but cried and made a fuss till I took him down the drive again. And it wasn't so much that he seemed happy in the field as anxious to be there. And there was he in a wood all the time and me in a field. It seemed to me I ought to mention it to his Lordship. So I did, and for a moment
10 he looked away from me, as if he was upset and not sure what to say. And then he said, 'Have you tried to keep him away from there?' And I said I had but that it wasn't any use. And he said, 'Well, then—' and he paused for a bit. 'Well, then, let him play there, but don't let him wander off by himself.' I was sorry I'd told him in a way, but I thought I ought to."

"What was the field like? Were there stumps of trees there? Had it been a wood?"

"No, it was just an ordinary grass field."

20   "Did you see any birds or animals in it?"

"No; why do you ask that?"

"I don't know exactly."

"Well, it's a fact I never saw bird or beast in that field except a dead rabbit once. The gardener picked it up and had a look at it, but he couldn't find anything wrong with it, so he said it must have died of old age, and he threw it away. Master Jocelyn was always drawing pictures of a wood, and he was clever at it and made it look real. But he always drew the same one with
30 a big tree in the middle. But he couldn't seem to draw the big tree properly, but always made a red and black smudge around it. And it was a funny thing how he

was: were □ **worry me:** make me anxious
get him past...: make him go past...without stopping
wouldn't: refused to □ **tried (+ ing):** employed the method of
cried: let water fall from his eyes
fuss: scene
it wasn't so much...: he appeared more anxious than happy
there was he: there he was □ **wood:** little forest
ought to: should

away: in another direction □ **upset:** troubled
tried (+ to): made an effort to
keep him away: maintain him at a distance
wasn't any use: wasn't successful
paused: stopped speaking □ **bit:** moment
wander off: walk away □ **by himself:** unaccompanied
in a way: to a certain degree □ **I ought to:** it was my duty
what...like: describe the field to me □ **stump(s):** part left in the
ground when you cut down a tree

bird(s): a cuckoo is a bird

beast: animal
dead: ≠ living □ Bugs Bunny is a **rabbit!** □ **picked:** took
had a look at: examined
wrong: showing it was ill or had been hurt □ **must have:** very
probably had □ **threw it away:** didn't keep it
drawing: making; draw, drew, drawn □ **clever (at!):** good (at!)
look: appear □ **same:** identical
seem: appear
properly: correctly
smudge: dirty mark □ **funny:** strange

always made straight for the place where that big tree would have been if there had been a wood, and then he'd look up. And he used to pick his way along as if he was dodging trees, and following some sort of pathway. He talked very little and always seemed to be thinking his own thoughts. He grew up into the most lovely little boy. He learnt his lessons all right, but not as if he cared so much about them, though he was very quick and sharp about some things."

10   "When he was in the field, could he see you?"

"What questions you ask! Well, I can't be sure; he never looked at me or said a word. He just wandered about, and I got out of the way of speaking to him, though I always kept an eye on him."

"Did it put the wind up you?"

"There you are with your vulgar talk! I always felt a bit uneasy, but I got used to it and didn't bother as a rule. But sometimes when I got drowsy and day-dreaming I'd think for a second or two I *was* in a wood
20 and hearing a sort of rustle of leaves, and get a feeling that someone was watching me; but then I'd come to myself and know I'd been imagining things. We lived a very quiet life, with just a break of six weeks every summer when we went to Bognor—the doctor said the air there was good for Master Jocelyn. He seemed to like the seaside, though I couldn't get him to make friends with other children. But he liked his bathe and sitting on the beach and watching the water. And he loved the boats."

30   "You don't see any decent liners at Bognor, only dull old tramps. Deal's the place."

"Oh, well, he wasn't so particular, nor such a Johnny-

made straight for: went directly to

pick his way: advance slowly and prudently
dodging: going round □ **following:** taking □ **pathway:** route

grew up: developed □ **lovely:** attractive
all right: well □ **cared...about:** was really interested in

sharp: intellectually alert

wandered about: walked about with no particular intention
way: habit
though: although, even if
put the wind up: (sb.) frighten, terrify

uneasy: ill at ease □ **used:** accustomed □ **bother:** worry □ **as a rule:** in general □ **got drowsy...day-dreaming:** felt a bit somnolent and fell into a reverie
rustle: trembling sound □ **leaves** fall in autumn □ **feeling:** impression □ **come to myself:** become fully conscious again

break: interruption, holiday
Bognor Regis is a seaside town in West Sussex

seaside: where the land meets the sea (= ocean) □ **get:** persuade □ **bathe:** bath in the sea
holidaymakers sunbathe in bikinis on a **beach**
boat(s): ship
decent: real □ **liner(s):** luxurious passenger ship □ **dull:** uninteresting □ **tramp(s):** cargo-boat □ **Deal:** town in Kent, ideal place to see liners □ **particular:** difficult to please

Know-all as you. But I believe he was nearly always thinking of the wood. He used to try and draw it on the sand with a shell.

"Things went on much the same till just after his fifth birthday, and then I felt more bothered about him, for I got the idea that he was seeing someone in the field."

"Why did you think that, Nurse?"

"Now, wasn't I just going to tell you, impatient? Well, mostly from the way he stared and looked about him.
10 He seemed to be following something around—watching it. And as he didn't look up or down I took it that it was something or someone about his own size. I asked him what it was, though I never liked to put questions about the field. He didn't answer, but looked away from me. I felt it was a sort of secret of his and that I was left out of it.

"His Lordship asked me now and again how I found him, and I had to say he was a queer little chap, though as good as gold. I still love him, the sweet angel!"
20 "Better than me?"

"Well, you're not too bad, Master Gilbert, when you try to behave, which isn't often. Now, stop rubbing your toes together, those shoes have got to last you.

"I could see the master knew what I meant when I said, 'queer'. He looked as if there was nothing to be done. He used to spend an hour or two a day with Master Jocelyn, but I don't believe they was quite easy together. The little boy was fond of him and liked sitting on his knee or lying back against his shoulder, but it
30 was always the same story, he thought his own thoughts, and neither his father nor me came into them much of the time. And I think his Lordship knew that and felt

Johnny-Know-all: one who thinks he knows everything □
nearly: practically
children build **sand-**castles on the beach □ **shell:** hard exterior
of molluscs □ **things...same:** he continued to act more or less as
before □ **bothered:** anxious, worried □ **for:** because

mostly: principally □ **from:** because of □ **stared:** had an
absorbed expression □ **following** (with his eyes)
as: because □ **took it:** concluded
about his own size: more or less as tall as he was; what size are
you? What size of shoe do you take?

felt: had the impression
left out of: excluded from
now and again: from time to time, occasionally
little chap: (fam.) boy
as...gold: a perfect little gentleman □ **sweet:** adorable

behave: act correctly □ **rubbing...toes:** continually pressing the
ends of your shoes □ **last you:** be durable
meant: wanted to say

spend: pass
was: were □ **quite:** completely □ **easy:** at ease, relaxed
was fond of: felt affection for
knee: joint in the leg □ **against:** on □ **shoulder:** joins arm to
body
came into them: occupied his thoughts

badly about it; and I used to get the idea that he'd given up hope, though he'd hardly confess it to himself. Layton seemed to make him worried and he used to spend a lot of time in London. He looked ill and tired and restless. But when Master Jocelyn's sixth birthday came near he stayed in the house, and, of course, I knew why. I kept the little boy near me night and day—it made me dream and sleep badly, for I had a feeling that the trouble was coming."

10   "What sort of trouble?"

"Well, haven't I told you about the curse and what always happened?"

"Yes, but—"

"Now, then, you're interrupting again. I just felt that I'd got to see that Master Jocelyn had someone on his side and fighting for him and that it wouldn't be my fault if the curse worked again. As the birthday drew near, his Lordship was like a cat on hot bricks, and I could have screamed sometimes, my nerves were so on

20 edge. His birthday was on March 21st. During the week before we'd been in the field every day and I'd watched him like a knife. March 20th was a very wild and windy day and Master Jocelyn seemed restless and broody, but all the same, when we went out in the afternoon I felt the worst was over, for what could happen between then and midnight? It was very dark for that time of year. Now, I don't know how to explain it, but as soon as we'd gone into the field everything seemed strange, as if it *was* a wood, and I thought I heard the trees fighting

30 with the wind, and for a bit I forgot Master Jocelyn, and I think I sat down and felt silly—as if I was someone else. And then, suddenly I heard a shout and

felt badly: had a bad conscience ☐ **given up:** abandoned
hope: all optimism ☐ **hardly...it:** confess it just a little

ill: not well ☐ **tired:** fatigued
restless: agitated, nervous; he could not rest
came near: approached ☐ **stayed in:** never left ☐ **of course:**
naturally

trouble: danger

curse: malediction ☐ **what always happened:** the fact that the
eldest son never lived to see his sixth birthday

felt: considered, was of the opinion that
see (to it): guarantee, ensure ☐ **on his side:** to protect him
fighting for: defending
worked: had its effect ☐ **drew near:** approached
like a cat...: extremely nervous and restless
screamed: emitted a piercing cry ☐ **my nerves were so on edge:** I
was so tense

like a knife: very attentively ☐ **wild and windy day:** a stormy
day when the wind blows violently ☐ **broody:** unhappily
ruminating
worst was over: most critical period has passed ☐ **then:** that
time ☐ **midnight:** 12 p.m. ☐ **it...dark:** there was practically no
sunlight ☐ **as soon as:** immediately after

was: really was ☐ **fighting:** battling
bit: some time ☐ **forgot:** neglected, did not think of
silly: strange
someone else: another person ☐ **shout:** cry

came to myself, and I couldn't see Master Jocelyn. So I
started to run, and I remember twisting and dodging as
if I was running through a wood, and I turned a corner,
and there was Master Jocelyn lying on his face, just
about where that big tree would have been. When I
reached him it was just a field again and he stretched
out on the grass. He was in a faint. I ran with him in
my arms back to the house. As I got near, his Lordship
came dashing out to meet me, and he took him from me
10 without a word. I was so out of breath that I had to lie
down on the lawn, and I thought my heart would burst.
As soon as I could manage it, I got to the house. His
Lordship was giving Master Jocelyn brandy in his study
and the footman was rushing off on his bicycle for the
doctor. And then his Lordship carried Master Jocelyn
up to my bedroom, where he slept. He was dead white
and his eyes was shut, but he couldn't keep still. He
kept twisting and throwing out his arms, and then he
began to mutter—on and on and on—and presently he'd
20 scream. When the doctor came he asked me what had
happened, and I told him, but he never looked at the
master. And then he pulled up Master Jocelyn's sleeves,
and I could see his little arms was burnt past the elbow.
And the doctor said nothing, but got me to fetch
bandages and vaseline, and we did all we could for the
little boy. But nothing we did was any good. He kept
twisting and shifting and throwing out his arms and
always gave that scream. The doctor said he wasn't
really in pain, for he was quite unconscious. Just before
30 twelve o'clock he cried out, 'Mummie!' very loud three
times—and died.

"I can still remember how the wind was roaring, and

came to myself: recovered full consciousness
twisting...dodging: turning left and right in rapid succession, like a skier in a slalom

reached him: arrived where he was □ **stretched out:** lying fully extended □ **faint:** sort of coma

dashing: rushing, running
so out of breath: respiring with such difficulty
lawn: grass □ **heart:** pumping organ in body □ **burst:** explode
manage it: find the necessary energy □ **got:** went
brandy: cognac □ **study:** room for studying books and writing
footman: servant □ **rushing off:** riding away in haste
carried: transported
dead white: as white as death, very white
was: were □ **couldn't...still:** continued to move nervously
kept twisting: continued contorting his body □ **throwing out:** extending □ **mutter:** murmur □ **on...:** continuously □ **presently:** shortly after that

pulled: rolled □ **sleeve(s):** part of shirt covering arms
was: were □ **past:** above □ **elbow:** joint of arm
got: asked □ **fetch:** bring

any good: useful; what we did was no good
shifting: displacing his body

pain: suffering
cried out: exclaimed □ **very loud:** at the top of his voice
died: stopped living
roaring: making a loud sound like a lion

how when he cried out the wind seemed to catch his cry
and carry it far, far away.

"They buried him three days later. The master kept
himself shut up in his room all the time. The family had
a vault in Layton Church, and the coffin was taken to it
in a farm cart. The wind had gone by then and it was a
queer, dark, close afternoon, not a bit like any March
day I've ever seen. I remember I walked behind the cart
with the master, though otherwise I've always been a bit
10 hazy about that day. We had to go down the drive, for
the church was just off the main road. Well, just as we
reached the middle of that field something seemed to
flash down from the sky and there was a great flame
before my eyes. And I seemed to see Master Jocelyn
jump down from the cart and start to run along the
path through the wood. And I went after him. And it
was a wood this time, and very dark. But ahead I could
see a big red glare and, as I got near, flames above it.
And they came from the same spot by the big tree. And
20 all the time I could see Master Jocelyn running ahead of
me. And then I turned a corner, and there was a great
pile of flaming wood and I could hear it roaring. And I
seemed to be running through a big crowd of people
who made way for me. And Master Jocelyn ran straight
into the fire and disappeared. Then, just as I reached the
blaze I heard him scream and I saw his little arms flung
above the flames. And I tried to reach up to him, but
the flames came out at me—and the next thing I knew
was waking up at the Klerkley Cottage Hospital and
30 finding my arms all bandaged up and most of the hair
burnt off my head. I didn't understand what had
happened for a day or two because they wouldn't let me

catch: seize

buried him: placed him in the cemetery
shut up in: confined to
vault: large tomb □ **coffin:** box where dead body is placed
cart: vehicle □ **gone:** stopped □ **by then:** when the funeral
began □ **close:** warm and airless □ **not a bit:** in no way
behind: ≠ in front of
otherwise: except for that detail
hazy: uncertain
church: religious edifice □ **off:** next to □ **main:** principal

sky: the sun shines in the sky

jump down: descend quickly
path: little road
ahead: in front (of me)
glare: bright light □ **got near:** approached
spot: place □ **by:** near, beside

wood: combustible material from trees □ **roaring:** burning
intensely □ **crowd:** group
made way for me: let me pass □ **straight:** directly
fire: flames
blaze: brightly burning fire □ **flung:** extended desperately
reach up to him: extend my arms to seize him
came out at me: advanced in my direction
waking up: regaining consciousness □ **cottage hospital:** small
rural hospital □ **most of:** almost all

let me: permit me to

talk. But when I was better they told me I'd been struck by lightning and knocked down silly for three days, and that was really how I got the burns."

"But what happened to Lord Layton if he was walking beside you?"

"Now, don't you worry about that, because I'm not going to tell you. And I suppose you'll have dreams and I'll get the blame. But you pester so and you're always reading those horrid ghost books."

10   "But tell me, Nurse, why—"

"I shan't tell you another word. You get on with that drawing of the house while I wake Miss Dolly and take her some Benger's. And don't kick your toes together. Those shoes have got to last."

struck: hit; strike, struck, struck
lightning: electric flash from the sky □ **knocked down silly:** rendered prostrate and unconscious

beside: next to
worry about: concern yourself with

pester: insist harassingly □ **so:** so much
horrid: very unpleasant

get on with: continue
drawing: picture □ **while:** at the same time as □ **wake...:** stop Miss D. sleeping □ **Benger's:** medicinal tonic □ **kick...:** tap the front part of your shoes together violently

Grammaire au fil des nouvelles

En traduisant les phrases suivantes qui contiennent des difficultés grammaticales suggérées par les italiques, essayez de retrouver le texte anglais dont la page est indiquée par le premier chiffre et les lignes par les suivants; les chiffres en gras renvoient à la Grammaire active *de l'anglais publiée au Livre de Poche.*

Il est grand temps que tu le *fasses* (50. 16. p. 42).

Il y a environ vingt-cinq ans *que je suis allée* à Layton Hall pour la première fois (50. 28. p. 34).

Il y a bien longtemps on *a brûlé* une sorcière (52. 7-8. p. 34).

Il *ne* pleurait *presque jamais* (52. 21. p. 142).

Les bébés en bonne santé *devraient* pleurer (52. 22. p. 24).

Autrefois tu pleurais jusqu'au moment où j'*aurais pu* t'étrangler (52. 23. pp. 58, 26).

Cela ne m'aurait pas gêné (54. 3. p. 42).

Il *n'y* avait *personne* dans la cathédrale (54. 9. p. 78).

Il *insistait* toujours *pour sortir* (54. 23. p. 150).

Il *ne* me *laissait jamais faire* cela *non plus* (56. 4. pp. 62, 163).

Il a *dû mourir* de vieillesse (56. 26. p. 26).

Arrête de frotter les bouts de tes chaussures l'un contre l'autre (60. 22. p. 150).

Cela m'a *fait rêver et mal dormir* (62. 7-8. p. 62).

J'entendais les arbres *lutter* avec le vent (62. 29. p. 60).

Il *se tordait sans cesse* (64. 18. p. 150).

Il m'a demandé *ce qui* s'était passé (64. 20. p. 134).

J'ai *cru voir* Master Jocelyn *sauter* de la charrette (66. 14. p. 150).

Ils *n'ont pas voulu me laisser parler* (66. 32. p. 62).

The Ghost

by Richard Hughes (1900-1976)

A novelist, poet, playwright, historian and writer of children's stories, Richard Hughes also has the distinction of writing the first ever radio drama for the BBC in 1924. His most famous novel, *A High Wind in Jamaica* (1929) (in the American edition: *The Innocent Voyage*) was one of the first novels to take an unsentimental look at childhood. Although born in Surrey and educated at Oxford, he was proud of being a Welshman and spent most of his life on the Welsh coast which abounds in stories of haunted localities.

His typically Celtic interest in the supernatural inspired him to write several ghost stories, including the following one, taken from *A Moment in Time* (1926). Its psychological depth and doubly surprising ending make it no doubt his most original contribution.

He killed me quite easily by crashing my head on the cobbles. *Bang!* Lord, what a fool I was! All my hate went out with that first bang: a fool to have kicked up that fuss just because I had found him with another woman. And now he was doing this to me—*bang!* That was the second one, and with it *everything* went out.

My sleek young soul must have glistened somewhat in the moonlight: for I saw him look up from the body in a fixed sort of way. That gave me an idea: I would
10 haunt him. All my life I had been scared of ghosts: now I was one myself, I would get a bit of my own back. *He* never was: he said there weren't such things as ghosts. Oh, weren't there! I'd soon teach him. John stood up, still staring in front of him: I could see him plainly: gradually all my hate came back. I thrust my face close up against his: but he didn't seem to see it, he just stared. Then he began to walk forward, as if to walk through me: and I was afeard. Silly, for me—a spirit—to be afeard of his solid flesh: but there you are, fear
20 doesn't act as you would expect, ever: and I gave back before him, then slipped aside to let him pass. Almost he was lost in the street-shadows before I recovered myself and followed him.

And yet I don't think he could have given me the slip: there was still something between us that drew me to him—willy-nilly, you might say, I followed him up to High Street, and down Lily Lane.

Lily Lane was all shadows: but yet I could still see him as clear as if it was daylight. Then my courage came
30 back to me: I quickened my pace till I was ahead of him—turned round, flapping my hands and making a moaning sort of noise like the ghosts did I'd read of. He

killed me: caused my death □ **quite:** very □ **crashing:** breaking
cobble(s): round paving stone □ **fool:** idiot □ **hate:** ≠ love
went out: disappeared □ **bang:** explosive noise □ **kicked up that
fuss:** made such a scene □ **found:** discovered

sleek: bright □ **soul:** spirit □ **glistened:** shone □ **somewhat:** a
little □ **moonlight:** lunar light □ **look up:** ≠ look down
a fixed sort of way: a rather fixed way
scared: terrified □ **now (that) I was...**
a bit of my own back: a little of my revenge
he said...ghosts: he did not think that ghosts existed
weren't there: really! □ **soon:** in a short time
still staring: continuing to look fixedly □ **plainly:** clearly
thrust: pushed □ **close up against:** very near
seem: appear
walk forward: advance □ **walk through:** traverse
afeard: afraid □ **silly:** stupid
flesh: substance a body is made of □ **there you are:** in fact
expect: anticipate □ **gave back:** moved back a little
slipped aside: moved quickly to one side □ **almost:** nearly
shadow(s): dark place □ **recovered myself:** regained my self-
control □ **followed him:** walked behind him
and yet: all the same □ **given me the slip:** escaped from me
drew: attracted; draw, drew, drawn
willy-nilly: irresistibly, against my will
a **lane** is a little street

quickened my pace: walked faster □ **till:** until □ **ahead:** in front
flapping: moving up and down (like a bird's wings)
moaning: making a sad cry when suffering

began to smile a little, in a sort of satisfied way: but yet
he didn't seem properly to see me. Could it be that his
hard disbelief in ghosts made him so that he *couldn't* see
me? *"Hoo!"* I whistled through my small teeth. *"Hoo!
Murderer! Murderer!"*—Someone flung up a top window. "Who's that?" she called. "What's the matter?"—
So other people could hear, at any rate. But I kept
silent: I wouldn't give him away—not yet. And all the
time he walked straight forward, smiling to himself. He
10 never had any conscience, I said to myself: here he is
with new murder on his mind, smiling as easy as if it
was nothing. But there was a sort of hard look about
him, *all* the same.

It was odd, my being a ghost so suddenly, when ten
minutes ago I was a living woman: and now, walking on
air, with the wind clear and wet between my shoulder-
blades. Ha-ha! I gave a regular shriek and a screech of
laughter, it all felt so funny.... surely John must have
heard *that*: but no, he just turned the corner into Pole
20 Street.

All along Pole Street the plane-trees were shedding
their leaves: and then I knew what I would do. I made
those dead leaves rise up on their thin edges, as if the
wind was doing it. All along Pole Street they followed
him, pattering on the roadway with their five dry
fingers. But John just stirred among them with his feet,
and went on: and I followed him: for as I said, there
was still some tie between us that drew me.

Once only he turned and seemed to see me: there was
30 a sort of recognition in his face: but no fear, only
triumph. "You're glad you've killed me," thought I,
"but I'll make you sorry!"

smile: have an expression of pleasure on his face
properly: distinctly □ **could it be** (possible) that...
hard...ghosts: categorical refusal to accept ghosts as real
whistled: made a sound □ **teeth** are treated by the dentist
murderer: killer □ **flung up:** opened quickly □ **top:** upstairs
called: cried out □ **matter:** problem
other people: not just he and I □ **at any rate:** that was sure
give him away: denounce him to the police □ **not yet:** not now
straight forward: exactly in front of him
never: ≠ always
mind: conscience
nothing ≠ something □ **hard look about him:** severe expression
on his face □ **all the same:** at the same time
odd: strange □ **my being:** the fact that I was

wet: rain makes things wet □ **shoulder-blade(s):** *omoplate*
regular (fam.): real □ **shriek:** strident cry □ **screech of laughter:**
piercing mocking sound □ **funny:** amusing
corner: angle where streets meet

plane-tree(s): *platane* □ **shedding:** losing
leaves: (a leaf) trees shed their leaves in autumn
dead: ≠ living □ **thin:** fine □ **edge:** border, extremity
followed: went after
pattering: tapping □ **roadway:** middle of street □ **dry:** ≠ wet
finger(s): five fingers on a hand □ **stirred:** pushed □ **feet:** (a
foot) part of body to walk with □ **went on:** continued
tie: connection, link, bond
once: one time (once, twice, three times...)
recognition: expression showing he knew me □ **fear:** terror
glad: happy, contented
make you sorry: make you regret it

And then all at once the fit left me. A nice sort of
Christian, I, scarcely fifteen minutes dead and still
thinking of revenge, instead of preparing to meet my
Lord! Some sort of voice in me seemed to say: "Leave
him, Millie, leave him alone *before it is too late!*" Too
late? Surely I could leave him when I wanted to? Ghosts
haunt as they like, don't they? I'd make just one more
attempt at terrifying him: then I'd give it up and think
about going to heaven.

10   He stopped, and turned, and faced me full.

I pointed at him with both my hands.

"John!" I cried, "John! It's all very well for you to
stand there, and smile, and stare with your great fish-
eyes and think you've won: but you haven't! I'll do you.
I'll *finish* you! I'll—"

I stopped and laughed a little. Windows shot up.
"Who's that? What's the row?"—and so on. They had
all heard: but he only turned and walked on.

"Leave him, Millie, before it is too late," the voice
20 said.

So that's what the voice meant: leave him before I
betrayed his secret, and had the crime of revenge on my
soul. Very well, I would: I'd leave him. I'd go straight to
heaven before any accident happened. So I stretched up
my two arms, and tried to float into the air: but at once
some force seized me like a great gust, and I was swept
away after him down the street. There was something
stirring in me that still bound me to him.

Strange, that I should be so real to all those people
30 that thought me still a living woman: but he—who
had most reason to fear me, why, it seemed doubtful
whether he even saw me. And where was he going to,

all at once: suddenly □ **fit:** intense feeling □ **nice:** good
scarcely: only □ **still thinking:** continuing to think
instead of preparing: in place of preparations
Lord: God, supreme divinity □ **leave...him alone:** don't torment
him □ **before:** ≠ after □ **late:** ≠ early
when I wanted to (leave): notice the omission of the verb

attempt: effort □ **give it up:** abandon it
heaven: where saints and angels live
faced me full: looked at me face to face
both my hands: my two hands
it's all very well for you to stand there: you can stand...
fish-eyes: big, round eyes (like those of a fish in the sea)
won: triumphed; win, won, won □ **do:** (fam.) eliminate, kill

laughed: made an amused sound □ **shot up:** opened suddenly
row: clamour □ **and so on:** etc
walked on: continued to walk
voice: an opera singer has a beautiful voice

meant: signified
betrayed: revealed
soul: conscience □ **straight:** directly
happened: took place □ **stretched up:** extended
tried: made an effort to □ **at once:** immediately
some: an unidentified □ **gust:** wind □ **swept away:** transported

stirring: moving □ **still bound:** continued to connect

fear: be terrified by □ **why:** well □ **doubtful:** uncertain
whether: if □ **even:** effectively

right up the desolate long length of Pole Street?—He turned into Rope Street. I saw a blue lamp: that was the police station.

"Oh, Lord," I thought, "I've done it! Oh, Lord, he's going to give himself up!"

"You drove him to it," the voice said. "You fool, did you think he didn't see you? What did you expect? Did you think he'd shriek, and gibber with fear at you? Did you think your John was a coward?—Now his death is
10 on your head!"

"I didn't do it, I didn't!" I cried. "I never wished him any harm, never, not *really*! I wouldn't hurt him, not for anything, I wouldn't. Oh, John, don't stare like that. There's still time... time!"

And all this while he stood in the door, looking at me, while the policemen came out and stood round him in a ring. He couldn't escape now.

"Oh, John," I sobbed, "forgive me! I didn't mean to do it! It was jealousy, John, what did it... because I
20 loved you."

Still the police took no notice of him.

"That's her," said one of them in a husky voice. "Done it with a hammer, she done it... brained him. But, Lord, isn't her face ghastly? Haunted, like."

"Look at her 'ead, poor girl. Looks as if she tried to do herself in with the 'ammer, after."

Then the sergeant stepped forward.

"Anything you say will be taken down as evidence against you."

30   "John!" I cried softly, and held out my arms—for at last his face had softened.

"Holy Mary!" said one policeman, crossing himself.

right: directly □ **desolate:** deserted □ **long length:** complete distance

done it: made a grave error
give himself up: confess his crime to the police
drove: forced; drive, drove, driven

shriek: cry □ **gibber:** talk fast in a confused manner
coward: ≠ courageous man □ **his death...head:** you will be responsible for his execution
wished him any harm: wanted to cause him any suffering
hurt: inflict pain on □ **not for anything:** not for the world

while: time
while: and during that time
ring: circle □ **escape:** run away
sobbed: said with emotion □ **forgive:** pardon □ **mean:** intend
what: (incorrect) that

took no notice of: paid no attention to
husky: raucous
done: did □ **hammer:** used for hitting things □ **brained him:** smashed his head □ **ghastly:** spectral □ **like:** you might say
'ead / 'ammer: dialectal pronunciation □ **looks:** (it) appears
do herself in: commit suicide
stepped forward: advanced a little, took a step forward
taken down: noted □ **evidence:** proof

softly: with little sound □ **held out:** extended
at last: finally □ **had softened:** had a gentler expression
holy: saint □ **crossing himself:** making the sign of the cross

"She's seeing him!"

"They'll not hang her," another whispered. "Did you notice her condition, poor girl?"

hang her: execute her by suspension □ **whispered:** murmured
notice her condition: see that she's pregnant, in the family way,
expecting (going to have) a baby!

Grammaire au fil des nouvelles

En traduisant les phrases suivantes qui contiennent des difficultés grammaticales suggérées par les italiques, essayez de retrouver le texte anglais dont la page est indiquée par le premier chiffre et les lignes par les suivants ; les chiffres en gras renvoient à la Grammaire active *de l'anglais publiée au* Livre de Poche.

Il me tua *en me fracassant la tête* (72. 1).

Quelle idiote j'étais (72. 2. **p. 66**).

Ma jeune âme *a dû briller* (72. 7. **p. 26**).

Je le vis *lever les yeux* (72. 8. **p. 60**).

Il avançait *comme pour me traverser* (72. 17-18. **p. 161**).

Je ne crois pas qu'il *aurait pu m'échapper* (72. 24. **p. 26**).

Je le *voyais* toujours *aussi* nettement *que* si l'on était en plein jour (72. 28-29. **pp. 60, 114**).

Il y a dix minutes j'étais une femme bien vivante (74. 14-15. **p. 34**).

John a *dû* sûrement *entendre* cela (74. 18. **p. 26**).

Je pensais à ma vengeance *au lieu de me préparer à* rencontrer mon Seigneur (76. 3. **p. 163**).

Les fantômes vous hantent *comme* ils veulent, *n'est-ce pas ?* (76. 7. **p. 46**).

Je lui ai fait signe *des deux mains* (76. 11. **p. 90**).

C'était bizarre que je *sois tellement* réelle (76. 29.).

Je *n'avais pas l'intention de le faire* (78. 18).

« C'est elle », dit l'un *d'entre eux, d'*une voix rauque (78. 22).

*On dirait qu'*elle *a essayé de* se supprimer (78. 25-26).

Dual Control

by *Elizabeth Walter* (1927-)

Elizabeth Walter is one of Britain's post-war specialists in the art of the ghost story. She has published a
number of volumes, including *Showfall* (1965), *The Sin
Eater* (1967), *Davy Jones's Tale* (1971), *Come and Get me*
(1973), and *Dead Woman* (1975), from which the
following story is taken.

Its title is an allusion to the fact that, when you learn
to drive, the instructor has dual controls to control the
car if you make a mistake. In this very modern and
highly dramatic ghost story the author plays on the
notion of "dual control" by presenting a diabolical duet
between a man and his wife, whose destiny, like the car
they are driving in, gets out of control, or rather,
becomes controlled by someone else, though not, of
course, an instructor!

"You ought to have stopped."

"For God's sake, shut up, Freda."

"Well, you should have. You ought to have made sure she was all right."

"Of course she's all right."

"How do you know? You didn't stop to find out, did you?"

"Do you want me to go back? We're late enough as it is, thanks to your fooling about getting ready, but I
10 don't suppose the Bradys'll notice if we're late. I don't suppose they'll notice if we never turn up, though after the way you angled for that invitation. . ."

"That's right, blame it all on me. We could have left half an hour ago if you hadn't been late home from the office."

"How often do I have to tell you that business isn't a matter of nine to five?"

"No, it's a matter of the Bradys, isn't it? You were keen enough we should get asked. Where were you
20 anyway? Drinking with the boys? Or smooching with some floozie?"

"Please yourself. Either could be correct."

"If you weren't driving, I'd hit you."

"Try something unconventional for a change."

"Why don't you try remembering I'm your wife—"

"Give me a chance to forget it!"

"—and that we're going to a party where you'll be expected to behave."

"I'll behave all right."

30   "To me as well as to other women."

"You mean you'll let me off the leash?"

"Oh, you don't give a damn about *my* feelings!"

ought to have: should have
God's sake: the love of God □ **shut up:** keep quiet (impolite)
made sure: verified
all right: well, not hurt
of course: naturally
find out: verify, check

late enough: sufficiently late
thanks...ready: because you spent too much time preparing
notice: realise
turn up: appear □ **though:** although, even if
angled for: employed various ruses to obtain
blame...me: say I'm responsible

office: room where boss and secretaries work
business: commercial affairs
matter of nine to five: question of having regular working hours
the Bradys: s! (Mr and Mrs Brady); the Laws...!
keen: enthusiastic □ **get asked:** be invited
anyway: now that I think of it □ **smooching:** (sl.) flirting
intimately □ **floozie:** (sl.) vulgar, immoral woman
please yourself: choose as you like □ **either:** one or the other

try: propose □ **for a change:** for once

expected to behave: supposed to conduct yourself correctly, to
be well-behaved □ **all right:** I assure you

mean: want to say □ **let...leash:** give me my liberty (like
detaching a dog from its chain) □ **give...about:** consider

"Look, if it hadn't been for you, I should have stopped tonight."

"Yes, you'd have given a pretty girl a lift if you'd been on your own. I believe you. The trouble is, she thought you were going to stop."

"So I was. Then I saw she was very pretty, and— Christ, Freda, you know what you're like. I've only got to be polite to a woman who's younger and prettier than you are—and believe me, there are plenty of them—and
10 you stage one of your scenes."

"I certainly try to head off the worst of the scandals. Really, Eric, do you think people don't know?"

"If they do, do you think they don't understand why I do it? They've only got to look at you... That's right, cry and ruin that fancy make-up. All this because I *didn't* give a pretty girl a lift."

"But she signalled. You slowed down. She thought you were going to... "

"She won't jump to conclusions next time."

20 "She may not jump at all. Eric, I think we ought to forget the Bradys. I think we ought to go back."

"To find Cinderella has been given a lift by Prince Charming and been spirited away to the ball?"

"She was obviously going to a party. Suppose it's to the Bradys' and she's there?"

"Don't worry, she couldn't have seen what we looked like."

"Could she remember the car?"

"No, she didn't have time."

30 "You mean she didn't have time before you hit her."

"God damn it, Freda, what do you expect me to do

look: look here (to draw attention to what you are saying)

pretty: attractive ☐ **given...lift:** taken...in your car
on...own: alone ☐ **believe you:** think you're right ☐ **trouble:** problem
so I was (going to stop): I really was going to stop
Christ: very impolite exclamation ☐ **what you're like:** how you normally conduct yourself
plenty: enough, a sufficient number
stage: make
head off: stop, prevent ☐ **worst:** most embarrassing; bad, worse, worst ≠ good, better, best
if they do: if they know

cry: let water come to your eyes ☐ **fancy make-up:** elaborate cosmetic preparation (powder, lipstick, eye-shadow)
slowed down: drove less quickly

jump to conclusions: react without waiting for confirmation
jump: move up and down

spirited away: transported as if by magic
obviously: manifestly
the Bradys' (party)
worry: be anxious ☐ **looked like:** resembled

remember: identify

hit: had a collision with

God damn it: expression of irritation ☐ **expect:** want

when a girl steps in front of the car just as I decide—for your sake—I'm not stopping? It wasn't much more than a shove."

"It knocked her over."

"She was off balance. It wouldn't have taken more than a touch."

"But she fell. I saw her go backwards. And I'm sure there was blood on her head."

"On a dark road the light's deceptive. You saw a
10 shadow."

"I wish to God I thought it was."

"Look here, Freda, pull yourself together. I'm sorry about it, of course, but it would make everything worse to go back and apologise."

"Then what are you stopping for?"

"So that you can put your face to rights and I can make sure the car isn't damaged."

"If it is, I suppose you'll go back."

"You underestimate me as usual. No, if it is I shall
20 drive gently into that tree. It will give us an excuse for arriving late at the Bradys' and explain the damage away."

"But the girl may be lying there injured."

"The road isn't that lonely, you know, and her car had obviously broken down. There'll be plenty of people willing to help a damsel in distress... Yes, it's as I thought. The car isn't even scratched. I thought we might have a dent in the wing, but it seems luck is on our side. So now, Freda, old girl, I'll have a nip from
30 that flask you've got in your handbag."

"I don't know what you mean."

"Oh yes you do. You're never without it, and it needs

steps: advances (by moving her foot = by taking a step) □ **for your sake:** out of consideration for your feelings
shove: push
knocked her over: made her fall down
was off balance: had lost her equilibrium □ **taken:** needed

go backwards: fall on her back (backwards ≠ forwards)
blood: red liquid in body □ **head:** part of body with face
dark: badly lit □ **(i)'s deceptive:** gives false impressions
shadow: dark form
to God: sincerely
pull...together: regain your self-control □ **'m sorry:** regret
worse: ≠ better
apologise: offer my excuses, say I'm sorry
what...for: why
put...to rights: arrange your make-up

as usual: as you habitually do
gently: slowly
explain...away: find a false explanation for

injured: damaged, hurt (in accident) ≠ wounded (in battle)
lonely: isolated, with little traffic
obviously: clearly □ **broken down:** stopped due to mechanical problem □ **willing:** prepared □ **damsel:** young lady
isn't...scratched: hasn't lost any paint
dent: damaged part □ **wing:** front side □ **luck:** good fortune
nip: little drink
flask: little bottle □ **handbag:** where women put everything!

a refill pretty often by now."

"I can't think what's come over you, Eric."

"Call it delayed shock. Are you going to give it me or do I have to help myself?"

"I can't imagine—Eric, let go! You're hurting!"

"The truth does hurt at times. Do you think I didn't know you had what's called a drinking problem? You needn't pretend with me."

"It's my money. I can spend it how I choose."

10 "Of course, my love. Don't stop reminding me that I'm your pensioner, but thanks anyway for your booze."

"I didn't mean that. Oh Eric, I get so lonely, you don't know. And even when you're home you don't take any notice of me. I can't bear it. I love you so."

"Surely you can't have reached the maudlin stage already? What are the Bradys going to think?"

"I don't give a damn about the Bradys. I keep thinking about that girl."

20 "Well, I give a damn about the Bradys. They could be important to me. And I'm not going to ruin a good contact because my wife develops sudden scruples."

"Won't it ruin it if they know you left a girl for dead by the roadside?"

"Maybe, but they won't know."

"They will. If you don't go back, I'll tell them."

"That sounds very much like blackmail, and that's a game that two can play."

"What do you mean?"

30 "Who was driving the car, Freda?"

"You were."

"Can you prove that?"

a refill: to be filled again with petrol □ **pretty:** rather
what's come over: what has affected
delayed shock: shock having its effect later than the accident
that caused it □ **help:** serve
let go: stop holding (the flask) □ **hurting:** causing pain
truth: reality □ **does hurt:** really hurts
had...drinking problem: were an alcoholic
pretend: dissimulate

reminding me: making me realise again
I'm your pensioner: I depend on you financially □ **anyway:** in
any case □ **booze:** (sl.) alcoholic drink(s)
lonely: without company

take...notice of: pay attention to □ **bear:** tolerate □ **so:** so much
reached...stage: arrived at the sentimental phase
already: in such a short time
I don't give a damn: I'm indifferent □ **keep:** cannot stop

I give a damn: I'm not indifferent

dead: ≠ living, alive (death ≠ life)

maybe: perhaps

sounds: appears by your tone of voice □ **blackmail:** menaces □
that's a game that two can play: I can act just as badly as you
(game: poker is a game)

"As much as you can prove that I was."

"Ah, but it's not as simple as that. Such an accusation
would oblige me to tell the police about your drinking.
A lot of unpleasant things would come out. I should
think manslaughter is the least you'd get away with, and
that could get you five years. Because please note that
apart from that swig I am stone cold sober, whereas
your blood alcohol is perpetually high. In addition,
you're in a state of hysteria. Who d'you think would be
10 believed—you or I?"

"You wouldn't do that, Eric. Not to your wife. Not to
me."

"Sooner than I would to anyone, but it won't come to
that, will it, my dear?"

"I've a good mind to—"

"Quite, but I should forget it."

"Eric, don't you love me at all?"

"For God's sake, Freda, not that now, of all times. I
married you, didn't I? Ten years ago you were a good-
20 looking thirty—"

"And you were a smart young salesman on the
make."

"So?"

"You needed capital to start your own business."

"You offered to lend it to me. And I've paid you
interest."

"And borrowed more capital."

"It's a matter of safeguarding what we've got."

"What we've got. That's rich! You hadn't a penny.
30 Eric, don't start the car like that. You may not be drunk
but anyone would think you are, the way you're driving.
No wonder you hit that girl. And it wasn't just a shove.

come out: be revealed □ **should think:** imagine, suppose
manslaughter: involuntary homicide □ **least...get away with:**
minimum inculpation □ **get you:** condemn you to
swig: drink □ **stone cold:** very □ **whereas:** but, on the contrary
high: considerable □ **in addition:** what is more

wife: spouse, conjugal partner (husband + wife = couple)

sooner: more easily □ **it won't come to that:** we shall not arrive
at such a situation
I've a good mind to: I'd like to
quite: don't continue □ **I should forget it** (if I were you) = you
should forget it □ **at all:** in any way, just a little
not...now, of all times: especially not at this moment
a good-looking (attractive) **thirty-**year old woman

smart: intelligent □ **salesman:** commercial representative □ **on
the make:** prepared to act without scruples to make money
so?: so what?, so what do you mean by saying that?
business: commerce
lend: give (with the guarantee of being reimbursed later)

borrowed: took on credit

that's rich!: that's the limit (that I can tolerate)!
drunk: ≠ sober

no wonder: it's not surprising (that)

I think you've killed her."

"For God's sake, Freda, shut up!"

"Well, it was a good party, wasn't it?"

"Yes."

"Moira Brady's a marvellous hostess."

"Yes."

"Jack Brady's a lucky man. We ought to ask them back some time, don't you think?"

10 "Yes."

"What's got into you? Cat got your tongue? You're a fine companion. We go to a terrific party and all you can say is Yes."

"I'm thinking about that girl."

"She was all right, wasn't she? Except for some mud on her dress. Did she say anything about it?"

"She said she'd fallen over."

"She was speaking the literal truth. Now I hope you're satisfied I didn't hurt her!"

20 "She certainly looked all right."

"You can say that again. Life and soul of the party, and obviously popular."

"You spent enough time with her."

"Here we go again. Do you have to spend the whole evening watching me?"

"I didn't, but every time I looked, you were with her."

"She seemed to enjoy my company. Some women do, you know."

30 "Don't torment me, Eric. I've got a headache."

"So have I, as a matter of fact. Shall I open a window?"

killed her: caused her death

lucky: privileged □ **ask them back:** return their invitation
some time: some day, one day

got into: affected □ **cat got your tongue:** have you lost the capacity to speak □ **fine:** very good (ironic) □ **terrific:** very good (≠ terrible = very bad!)

mud: mixture of soil and water
dress: women wear long dresses at the opera
over: backwards, on her back
literal truth: exact reality □ **hope:** suppose (ironic)

you can...again: that's undeniable □ **life and soul...party:** the most amusing person at the party

here we go again: we've come back to the same subject
watching: observing, keeping an eye on

enjoy: like

headache: a pain in my head, migraine
so have I: I have a headache, too □ **as a matter of fact:** to tell the truth

"If it isn't too draughty.... What's the girl's name?"

"Gisela."

"It suits her, doesn't it? How did she get to the Bradys'?"

"I didn't ask."

"It's funny, but I never saw her go."

"I did. She left early because she said something about her car having engine trouble. I suppose someone was giving her a lift."

"I wonder if her car's still there?"

"It won't be. She'll have got some garage to tow it away."

"Don't be too sure. They're not so keen on coming out at nights in the country, unless something's blocking the road."

"I believe you're right. That's it, isn't it—drawn up on the grass verge."

"Yes. And Eric, that's her. She's hailing us."

"And this time, I'm really going to stop."

"What on earth can have happened?"

"It looks like another accident. That's fresh mud on her dress."

"And fresh blood on her head! Eric, her face is all bloody!"

"It can't be as bad as it looks. She's not unconscious. A little blood can go a very long way. Just keep calm, Freda, and maybe that flask of yours will come in handy. I'll get out and see what's up.... It's all right, Gisela. You'll be all right. It's me, Eric Andrews. We met at the Bradys' just now. My dear girl, you're in a state. What in God's name happened? Has someone tried to murder you? Here, lean on me..."

draughty: full of draughts (currents of air)

suits: corresponds well to □ **get to:** arrive at

funny: strange □ **go:** go away, leave
early: ≠ late
engine trouble: problems with the motor

wonder: ask myself □ **'s still:** continues to be
got: asked □ **tow...away:** transport it by attaching a cable

they: garage mechanics □ **keen on:** interested in; I'm keen on
(playing) tennis □ **unless:** except when

believe: think □ **that's it:** that's the car □ **drawn up:** stopped
grass verge: border of road with green grass
hailing: calling; you hail a taxi

what on earth: what the devil, what ever □ **happened:** taken
place □ **looks like:** resembles

bloody: covered with blood
looks: appears
a little blood...way: one can survive with a little blood
that flask of yours: your flask; a friend of hers, mine etc □
come in handy: be useful □ **what's up:** what's the problem,
what's the matter
just now: a short time ago
state: terrible state, condition
tried: made an effort □ **murder:** kill □ **lean:** lay your body

"Eric, what's the matter? Why have you left her alone? Gisela..."

"Christ, Freda, shut that window! And make sure your door's locked."

"What is it? You look as if you'd seen a ghost."

"She *is* a ghost... Give me that flask... That's better."

"What do you mean—a ghost?"

"There's nothing there when you go up to her. Only a
10 coldness in the air."

"But that's nonsense. You can't see through her. Look, she's still standing there. She's flesh and blood— blood certainly."

"Is there blood on my hand?"

"No, but it's shaking."

"You bet it is. So am I. I tell you, Freda, I put out my hand to touch her—I *did* touch her—at least, I touched where she was standing—but she's got no body to touch."

20   "She had a body at the Bradys'."

"I wonder."

"Well, you should know. You hung around her all the evening, making a spectacle of yourself."

"I never touched her."

"I'll bet it wasn't for want of trying."

"Now I think of it, nobody touched her. She always seemed to stand a little apart."

"But she ate and drank."

"She didn't eat. She said she wasn't hungry. I don't
30 remember seeing a glass in her hand."

"Rubbish, Eric. I don't believe you. For some reason you don't want to help her. Are you afraid she'll

matter: problem

locked: closed with lock pressed down
ghost: phantom
*is***:** is really (note the use of italics for emphasis)

go up to: approach
coldness: sensation of cold; cold(ness) ≠ heat
you can't see through her: she's not transparent
flesh: cannibals eat human flesh

shaking: trembling
bet: can be sure □ **put out:** extended
did **touch:** really touched (note the use of the auxiliary for
emphasis)

hung around: stood at her side and were very attentive to her

for want of trying: because you didn't make an effort

wasn't hungry: didn't have an appetite

rubbish: nonsense □ **some:** an inexplicable
afraid: anxious

recognise the car?"

"She has recognised it. That's why she's there. We—
we must have killed her on the way to the party that
time when we nearly stopped."

"You mean when *you* nearly stopped. When you hit
her. Oh God, what are we going to do?"

"Drive on, I think. She can't hurt us."

"But she could get inside the car."

"Not if we keep the doors locked."

10   "Do you think locked doors can keep her out? Oh
God, I wish I'd never come with you. Oh God, get me
out of this. I never did anything. I wasn't driving. Oh
God, I'm not responsible for what he does."

"Oh no, you're not responsible for anything, are you,
Freda? Does it occur to you that if it hadn't been for
your damned jealousy I should have stopped?"

"You've given me cause enough for jealousy since we
were married."

"A man's got to get it somewhere, hasn't he? And
20 you were pretty useless—admit it. You couldn't even
produce a child."

"You're heartless—heartless."

"And you're spineless. A sponge, that's all you
are."

"I need a drink to keep me going, living with a
bastard like you."

"So we have to wait while you tank up and make
ourselves late for the Bradys'. Do you realise, if we'd
been earlier we shouldn't have seen that girl?"

30   "It's my fault again, is it?"

"Every bloody thing's your fault. I could have built
up the business a whole lot faster if you'd put yourself

recognise: identify

must have: very probably □ **on the way to:** when driving to
nearly: almost

drive on: continue to drive
get: come

keep...out: maintain her at a distance
get me out of this: help me out of this terrible situation

responsible for: note the preposition!

does it occur to you: do you realise
damned: detestable
cause enough: sufficient reasons

get it: have sexual relations
pretty: more or less
child: baby
heartless: without a heart, pitiless, unfeeling, cruel
spineless: with no backbone = without moral courage; an
invertebrate has no spine or backbone
keep me going: permit me to survive
bastard: sadistic, immoral person (improper)
tank up: drink a lot, get drunk; tank = container for liquid

is it: is that what you're insinuating
every bloody thing: the whole terrible situation (improper) □
built up: enlarged □ **a whole lot:** much □ **put yourself**

out to entertain a bit. If I'd had a wife like Moira
Brady, things would be very different from what they
are."

"You mean you'd make money instead of losing it."

"What do you mean—losing it?"

"I can read a balance sheet, you know. Well, you're
not getting any more of my money. 'Safeguarding our
interests' I don't think! Paying your creditors is more
like it."

10   "Now look here, Freda, I've had enough of this."

"So have I. But I'm not walking home so there's no
point in stopping."

"Then try getting this straight for a change—"

"Eric, there's that girl again."

"What are you talking about? Anyone would think
you'd got DTs."

"Look—she's bending down to speak to you. She's
trying to open your door."

"Christ!"

20   "Eric, don't start the car like that. Don't drive so
furiously. What are you trying to do?"

"I'm trying to outdistance her."

"But the speed limit..."

"Damn the speed limit! What's the good of having a
powerful car if you don't use it?... That's right. You
hit the bottle again."

"But the way you're driving! You ignored a halt sign.
That lorry driver had to cram on his brakes."

"What the hell! Look round and see if you can see
30 her."

"She's right behind us, Eric."

"What, in her car?"

out: made a real effort □ **entertain:** give parties □ **a bit:** a little

instead of losing: and not, on the contrary, lose

balance sheet: list of company's profits and losses

I don't think!: my eye! □ **is more like it:** corresponds more exactly to the facts
had...this: listened to you for a sufficiently long time
there's no point in: it's no use (it is useless, futile)

getting...straight: understanding this clearly

DTs: delirium tremens: illness among alcoholics causing hallucinations □ **bending down:** inclining forward

outdistance her: leave her behind at a great distance
speed limit: in towns it's 50 kms an hour in France, 30 miles per hour in Britain □ **what's...having:** why have; what is the use/point of + ing □ **powerful:** capable of going fast
hit the bottle: start drinking
ignored: paid no attention to □ **halt sign:** stop sign
lorry: vehicle for transporting merchandise □ **cram...brakes:** press brake pedal violently □ **what the hell:** I don't give a damn!
right: just □ **behind:** ≠ in front of
what: what do you mean?

"No, she seems to be floating a little way above the ground. But she's moving fast. I can see her hair streaming out behind her."

"Well, we're doing seventy-five ourselves."

"But we can't go on like this for ever. Sooner or later we've got to get out."

"Sooner or later she's got to get tired of this caper."

"Where are we? This isn't the way home."

10   "Do you want her following us home? I want to lose her. What do you take me for?"

"A bastard who's ruined my life and ended that poor girl's."

"No one warned me you'd ruin mine. I wish they had. I might have listened. Warnings are only given to the deaf... Look again to see if Gisela's still following."

"She's just behind us. Oh Eric, her eyes are wide and staring. She looks horribly, horribly dead. Do you suppose she'll ever stop following us? Gisela. It's a form
20 of Giselle. Perhaps she's like the girl in the ballet and condemned to drive motorists to death instead of dancers."

"Your cultural pretensions are impressive. Is your geography as good?"

"What do you mean?"

"I mean where the hell are we? I swear I've never seen this road before. It doesn't look like a road in southern England. More like the North Yorkshire moors, except that even there there's some habitation. Besides, we
30 couldn't have driven that far."

"There's a signpost at this next crossroads if you'll slow down enough for me to read..."

seems: appears □ **way:** distance

streaming out: floating horizontally in the wind
seventy-five: 75 mph (miles per hour) = 120 km/h
go on: continue □ **ever:** always □ **sooner or later:** at one time
or another in the future
get tired of: abandon all interest in
caper: stupid manner of acting
the way home: the direction for home
want her (to be) **following** □ **lose:** outdistance

ended...girl's (life): put an end to her life, killed her

warned me: told me of the danger that □ **wish...had:** regret they
didn't □ **warning(s):** danger signal
the deaf: people who cannot hear (a deaf person)
wide: fully open
staring: looking fixedly □ **dead:** ≠ living, alive

Giselle: principal character in the ballet by Adam
drive...to death: force to die □ **instead of:** in place of

the hell: (where) ever, on earth, the devil □ **swear:** solemnly
promise □ **southern:** the South of
North: ≠ South □ **Yorkshire:** region in England □ **moor(s):**
deserted region without trees □ **besides:** what is more
that far: as far as that
signpost: post indicating directions □ **crossroads:** junction where
two roads form a cross □ **enough:** sufficiently

"Well?"

"I don't understand it, Eric. All four arms of the signpost are blank."

"Vandals painted them out."

"Vandals! In this desolate, isolated spot? Oh Eric, I don't like this. Suppose we're condemned to go on driving for ever?"

"No, Freda, the petrol would give out."

"But the gauge has been at nought for ages. Hadn't
10 you noticed?"

"What? So it is. But the car's going like a bird."

"Couldn't you slow down a bit? I know you didn't for the signpost, but she—she's not so close behind us now... Please, Eric, my head's still aching."

"What do you think I'm trying to do?"

"But we're doing eighty... I knew it. We'll have to go on driving till we die."

"Don't be such an utter bloody fool. I admit we've seen a ghost—something I never believed existed. I
20 admit I've lost control of this damn car and I don't know how she keeps running on no petrol. I also admit I don't know where we are. But for all this there's got to be a rational explanation. Some time-switch in our minds. Some change of state."

"That's it! Eric, what's the last landmark you can remember?"

"That blanked-out signpost."

"Not that. I mean the last normal sign."

"You said there was a halt sign, but I must say I
30 never saw it."

"You drove right through it, that's why. We shot straight in front of a lorry. I think—oh Eric, I think

well: what could you read?
arms: people have two with hands on them
blank: not written on
painted...out: effaced them by covering them with paint
desolate: deserted □ **spot:** region
go on: continue, keep

petrol...out: there would be no more petrol (combustible liquid
for car engines) □ **nought:** zero □ **ages:** a very long time
noticed: observed
like a bird: easily, effortlessly like a bird flying

for the signpost: to consult the signpost □ **close:** near
aching: hurting, causing pain (headache, toothache)

till: until, up to the moment when
utter: total □ **bloody:** damned (improper) □ **fool:** imbecile

she keeps running: the engine continues to turn; "she" is used
for cars, boats and ships
time-switch: instrument that changes sth. from one time zone to
another □ **mind(s):** head
that's it: that's the solution □ **landmark:** object making
orientation possible
blanked-out: effaced

drove...it: crossed the white line without stopping □ **shot:** drove
very fast □ **straight:** directly

we're dead."

"Dead! You must be joking. Better have another drink."

"I can't. The flask's empty. Besides, the dead don't drink. Or eat. They're like Gisela. You can't touch them. There's nothing there."

"Where's Gisela now?"

"A long, long way behind us. After all, she's had her revenge."

10 "You're hysterical, Freda. You're raving."

"What do you expect but weeping and wailing? We're in Hell."

"The religious beliefs of childhood reasserting themselves."

"Well, what do you think Hell is? Don't hurry, you've got eternity to answer in. But I know what *I* think it is. It's the two of us driving on alone. For ever. Just the two of us, Eric. For evermore."

must...joking: can't be serious □ **you had better have:** you should have

empty: ≠ full (there's no alcohol left) □ **the dead:** dead people (a dead person) ≠ the living

raving: talking like someone who is mad, mentally deranged

expect: think to find □ **but:** except □ **weeping and wailing:** lamentations □ **Hell:** where the damned are tortured; ≠ heaven

belief(s): conviction □ **childhood:** ≠ adulthood □ **reasserting themselves:** coming back up to the surface

don't hurry: take your time

to answer in: during which you can answer

for ever: for always

for evermore: for ever and ever and ever !!!

Grammaire au fil des nouvelles

En traduisant les phrases suivantes qui contiennent des difficultés grammaticales suggérées par les italiques, essayez de retrouver le texte anglais dont la page est indiquée par le premier chiffre et les lignes par les suivants ; les chiffres en gras renvoient à la Grammaire active *de l'anglais publiée au Livre de Poche.*

Tu *aurais dû t'arrêter !* (84. 1. pp. **24, 26**).

Veux-tu *que j'y retourne ?* (84. 8. p. **54**).

On est *assez en retard* comme ça (84. 8. p. **140**).

Nous *aurions pu* partir *il y a* une heure si tu *n'étais pas rentré* tard du bureau (84. 13-15. pp. **26, 34, 42**).

Combien de fois faut-il que je te dise... (84. 16. pp. **144, 22**).

Si tu *n'étais pas en train de conduire,* je te *frapperais* (84. 23. p. **42**).

Une réception où *on s'attendra à ce que tu te conduises bien* (84. 27-28. p. **54**).

Il se peut qu'elle soit étendue par terre là-bas (88. 23. p. **26**).

Inutile de faire semblant avec moi (90. 8. p. **26**).

N'arrête surtout pas de me rappeler que je vis à tes crochets (90. 10. p. **150**).

Il est impossible que tu aies atteint le stade pleurnichard (90. 16. p. **26**).

Je *ne cesse de penser* à cette fille (90. 18-19. p. **150**).

A t'entendre on dirait vraiment du chantage (90. 27.).

Cela n'ira pas jusque-là, *n'est-ce pas ?* (92. 13-14. p. **46**).

Je ne l'ai pas du tout vue *partir* (96. 6. p. **60**).

Elle *l'aura fait remorquer par un garage quelconque* (96. 12. p. **62**).

Elle tremble !... *Moi aussi !* (98. 15. p. **48**).

Je ne me souviens pas *de l'avoir vue* un verre *à la main* (98. 30. p. **150**).

Nous *avons dû la tuer* (100. 3. p. **26**).

Je *regrette d'être venue* avec toi ! (100. 11. p. **42**).

La jauge *est* à zéro *depuis* une éternité (106. 9. pp. **32, 34**).

Midnight Express

by *Alfred Noyes* (1880-1958)

Born in Wolverhampton, educated in Wales and at Oxford, Alfred Noyes wrote many volumes of poetry but is best known for some traditional short poems like *The Highwayman*, a stirring romantic ballad that is also a ghost story and a favourite with school anthologies. Ghosts figure largely in his poetry, and fantasy dominates his collections of short stories which include *Walking Shadows* (1918) and *The Hidden Player* (1924).

His poetic talent for creating atmosphere is clearly revealed in this terrifying "story within a story", which starts with the familiar childhood experience of being afraid of a picture in a book and develops into a nightmarish vision of man's relation to the forces of destiny.

It was a battered old book, bound in red buckram.
He found it, when he was twelve years old, on an upper
shelf in his father's library; and, against all the rules, he
took it to his bedroom to read by candlelight, when the
rest of the rambling old Elizabethan house was flooded
with darkness. That was how young Mortimer always
thought of it. His own room was a little isolated cell, in
which, with stolen candle ends, he could keep the
surrounding darkness at bay, while everyone else had
10 surrendered to sleep and allowed the outer night to
come flooding in. By contrast with those unconscious
ones, his elders, it made him feel intensely alive in every
nerve and fibre of his young brain. The ticking of the
grandfather clock in the hall below, the beating of his
own heart; the long-drawn rhythmical "ah" of the sea
on the distant coast, all filled him with a sense of
overwhelming mystery; and, as he read, the soft thud of
a blinded moth, striking the wall above the candle,
would make him start and listen like a creature of the
20 woods at the sound of a cracking twig.

The battered old book had the strangest fascination
for him, though he never quite grasped the thread of the
story. It was called *The Midnight Express*, and there was
one illustration, on the fiftieth page, at which he could
never bear to look. It frightened him.

Young Mortimer never understood the effect of that
picture on him. He was an imaginative, but not a
neurotic youngster; and he avoided the fiftieth page as
he might have hurried past a dark corner on the stairs
30 when he was six years old, or as the grown man on the
lonely road, in *The Ancient Mariner*, who, having once
looked round, walks on, and turns no more his head.

battered: damaged □ **bound...buckram:** with a cover of red jute
upper: high (≠ lower)
shelf: plank □ **library:** book collection □ **against...rules:**
contrary to...regulations □ **candlelight** ≠ electric light
rambling: vast □ Queen **Elizabeth I** (1558-1603) □ **flooded**
...darkness: full of obscurity □ **young Mortimer:** no article!
own: personal □ **little:** small □ a prisoner lives in a **cell**
stolen: taken furtively □ **end(s):** small piece
surrounding: encircling □ **at bay:** at a distance □ **...else:** all the
others □ **surrendered:** capitulated □ **allowed...night:** permitted
the night outside □ **come flooding in:** invade the house
elder(s): senior □ **alive:** conscious, aware
brain: cerebral organ of intelligence □ **ticking:** tick-tock
a big **grandfather clock** stands on the floor □ **below:** downstairs □ **heart:** *cœur* □ **long-drawn:** prolonged □ **sea:** ocean
coast: where land meets sea □ **filled...with:** made him full of
overwhelming: all-enveloping □ **soft:** light □ **thud:** sound
blinded: *aveuglé* □ **moth:** night butterfly □ **striking:** hitting
start: react nervously
wood(s): small forest □ **twig:** very small branch

though: even if □ **quite:** entirely □ **grasped...thread:** understood
the line of development □ **midnight:** 12 p. m. (≠ midday)

bear: endure □ **frightened:** terrified

youngster: young boy □ **avoided:** refused to look at □ **as:** in the
same manner as □ **hurried:** ran □ **corner:** angle □ **stairs:** to go
up and down in a house □ **grown man:** adult
lonely: deserted □ *The Ancient Mariner*: ballad by the poet
Coleridge □ **round:** behind him □ **walks on:** continues to walk

There was nothing in the picture—apparently—to account for his haunting dread. Darkness, indeed, was almost its chief characteristic. It showed an empty railway platform—at night—lit by a single dreary lamp: an empty railway platform that suggested a deserted and lonely junction in some remote part of the country. There was only one figure on the platform: the dark figure of a man, standing almost directly under the lamp with his face turned away towards the black mouth of a
10 tunnel which—for some strange reason—plunged the imagination of the child into a pit of horror. The man seemed to be listening. His attitude was tense, expectant, as though he were awaiting some fearful tragedy. There was nothing in the text, so far as the child read, and could understand, to account for this waking nightmare. He could neither resist the fascination of the book, nor face that picture in the stillness and loneliness of the night. He pinned it down to the page facing it with two long pins, so that he should not come upon it by
20 accident. Then he determined to read the whole story through. But, always, before he came to page fifty, he fell asleep; and the outlines of what he had read were blurred; and the next night he had to begin again; and again, before he came to the fiftieth page, he fell asleep.

He grew up, and forgot all about the book and the picture. But halfway through his life, at that strange and critical time when Dante entered the dark wood, leaving the direct path behind him, he found himself, a little
30 before midnight, waiting for a train at a lonely junction; and, as the station-clock began to strike twelve he remembered; remembered like a man awakening from a

account for: explain □ **dread:** terror □ **indeed:** certainly
almost: more or less □ **chief:** principal □ **empty:** deserted
platform: where you get on trains □ **single:** unique □ **dreary:** lugubrious
junction: intersection □ **remote:** isolated
only: just □ **figure:** silhouette

turned away from the reader □ **towards:** to □ **mouth:** orifice

pit: abyss
seemed: appeared □ **tense:** full of tension □ **expectant:** excited
though: if □ **awaiting:** waiting for □ **fearful:** terrifying
so far as: as long as
waking nightmare: horrible vision seen when awake ≠ asleep

face: confront □ **stillness:** silence □ **loneliness:** solitude
pinned...down: attached it with a pin *(épingle)* □ **facing:** opposite
come upon it: open the book at that page
then: after that □ **whole:** entire
through: from beginning to end
fell asleep: began to sleep □ **outline(s):** contour
blurred: indistinct

grew up: became an adult, a grown-up □ **forgot:** ≠ remembered
halfway through: in the middle of
Dante...: allusion to *The Divine Comedy* □ **leaving:** abandoning
path: route □ **behind:** ≠ in front of

strike twelve: sound the twelve strokes of midnight
awakening: awaking, waking, waking up ≠ falling asleep

long dream—

There, under the single dreary lamp, on the long
glimmering platform, was the dark and solitary figure
that he knew. Its face was turned away from him
towards the black mouth of the tunnel. It seemed to be
listening, tense, expectant, just as it had been thirty-eight
years ago.

But he was not frightened now, as he had been
in childhood. He would go up to that solitary figure,
10 confront it, and see the face that had so long been
hidden, so long averted from him. He would walk up
quietly, and make some excuse for speaking to it: he
would ask it, for instance, if the train was going to be
late. It should be easy for a grown man to do this; but
his hands were clenched, when he took the first step,
as if he, too, were tense and expectant. Quietly, but
with the old vague instincts awaking, he went towards
the dark figure under the lamp, passed it, swung round
abruptly to speak to it; and saw—without speaking,
20 without being able to speak—

It was himself—staring back at himself—as in some
mocking mirror, his own eyes alive in his own white
face, looking into his own eyes, alive—

The nerves of his heart tingled as though their own
electric currents would paralyse it. A wave of panic went
through him. He turned, gasped, stumbled, broke into a
blind run, out through the deserted and echoing ticket-
office, on to the long moonlit road behind the station.
The whole countryside seemed to be utterly deserted.
30 The moonbeams flooded it with the loneliness of their
own deserted satellite.

He paused for a moment, and heard, like the echo of

dream: vision seen when asleep

glimmering: shining feebly and intermittently

in childhood: when he was a child ☐ **go up to:** approach

hidden: invisible ☐ **averted:** turned away ☐ **walk up:** advance
quietly: calmly
instance: example

clenched: closed firmly ☐ **took...step:** made the first movement
to advance
awaking: beginning to control him
swung round: pivoted
abruptly: suddenly

staring: looking fixedly
alive: full of life, intense

tingled: vibrated
wave: flowing movement like water ☐ **went through:** traversed
gasped: inhaled air nervously ☐ **stumbled:** almost fell ☐ **broke...**
run: suddenly began to run without looking about him
moonlit: full of lunar light
countryside: rural region ☐ **utterly:** completely
(moon)beam(s): ray ☐ **flooded:** inundated
satellite: moon
paused: stopped

his own footsteps, the stumbling run of something that
followed over the wooden floor within the ticket-office.
Then he abandoned himself shamelessly to his fear; and
ran, sweating like a terrified beast, down the long white
road between the two endless lines of ghostly poplars
each answering another, into what seemed an infinite
distance. On one side of the road there was a long
straight canal, in which one of the lines of poplars was
again endlessly reflected. He heard the footsteps echoing
10 behind him. They seemed to be slowly, but steadily,
gaining upon him. A quarter of a mile away, he saw a
small white cottage by the roadside, a white cottage with
two dark windows and a door that somehow suggested
a human face. He thought to himself that, if he could
reach it in time, he might find shelter and security—
escape.

The thin implacable footsteps, echoing his own, were
still some way off when he lurched, gasping, into the
little porch; rattled the latch, thrust at the door, and
20 found it locked against him. There was no bell or
knocker. He pounded on the wood with his fists until
his knuckles bled. The response was horribly slow. At
last, he heard heavier footsteps within the cottage.
Slowly they descended the creaking stair. Slowly the
door was unlocked. A tall shadowy figure stood before
him, holding a lighted candle, in such a way that he
could see little either of the holder's face or form; but to
his dumb horror there seemed to be a cerecloth wrapped
round the face.

30   No words passed between them. The figure beckoned
him in; and, as he obeyed, it locked the door behind
him. Then, beckoning him again, without a word, the

footstep(s): sound of walking □ **stumbling:** hesitant
followed: ran after □ **wooden floor:** parquet □ **within:** inside
shamelessly: without restraint □ **fear:** terror
sweating: perspiring □ **beast:** animal
endless: interminable □ **ghostly:** spectral □ **poplar(s):** *peuplier*
each...another: one...the other

straight: rectilinear

slowly: ≠ quickly □ **steadily:** progressively
quarter of a mile: four hundred metres
cottage: small house in the country
somehow: in an indefinable manner

reach: arrive at □ **shelter:** protection
escape: deliverance
thin: light □ **his own** footsteps □ **were still:** continued to be
some way off: at a distance □ **lurched:** almost fell
rattled...latch: pressed the bar nervously □ **thrust:** pushed
locked: shut with a key □ **bell:** to attract attention
knocker: *heurtoir* □ **pounded:** banged □ **wood:** *bois* □ **fist:** closed
hand □ **knuckle(s):** joint of finger □ **bled:** lost blood (liquid in
veins) □ **heavier:** more distinct; heavy ≠ light
creaking: making sound when under pressure
unlocked: opened □ **tall:** ≠ small □ **shadowy:** dark, spectral
holding in his hand □ **lighted:** burning □ **way:** manner
little: not much □ **(candle-)holder's face**
dumb: mute, silent □ **cerecloth:** used to **wrap round** (envelop) a
dead body
beckoned...in: signalled to him to enter

figure went before him up the crooked stair, with the
ghostly candle casting huge and grotesque shadows on
the whitewashed walls and ceiling.

They entered an upper room, in which there was a
bright fire burning, with an armchair on either side of it,
and a small oak table, on which there lay a battered old
book, bound in dark red buckram. It seemed as though
the guest had been long expected and all things were
prepared.

10   The figure pointed to one of the armchairs, placed the
candlestick on the table by the book (for there was no
other light but that of the fire) and withdrew without a
word, locking the door behind him.

Mortimer looked at the candlestick. It seemed familiar. The smell of the guttering wax brought back the
little room in the old Elizabethan house. He picked up
the book with trembling fingers. He recognised it at
once, though he had long forgotten everything about the
story. He remembered the ink stain on the title page;
20   and then, with a shock of recollection, he came on the
fiftieth page, which he had pinned down in childhood.
The pins were still there. He touched them again—the
very pins which his trembling childish fingers had used
so long ago.

He turned back to the beginning. He was determined
to read it to the end now, and discover what it all
was about. He felt that it must all be set down there, in
print; and, though in childhood he could not understand
it, he would be able to fathom it now.

30   It was called *The Midnight Express*; and, as he read
the first paragraph, it began to dawn upon him slowly,
fearfully, inevitably.

crooked: tortuous
casting: projecting □ **huge:** immense □ **shadow(s):** dark form
whitewashed: painted white □ **ceiling:** top of room
upper: upstairs
fire: in the chimney □ **armchair:** comfortable chair □ **either
side:** both sides □ **oak:** made of oak *(chêne)* □ **lay:** was

guest: invited person (Mortimer) □ **expected:** waited for

pointed to: indicated
candlestick: support for candle □ **by:** near, next to
but that: except the light □ **withdrew:** left the room

smell: odour □ **guttering wax:** burning candle □ **brought back:**
made him remember □ **picked up:** took
recognised: identified □ **at once:** immediately

ink: liquid to write with □ **stain:** mark □ **title page:** first page
recollection: remembering □ **came on:** arrived at

very: exact, same □ **childish:** very young

was...about: signified □ **set down...in print:** in typographical
characters
fathom it: elucidate the mystery of the story

it: the meaning of the story □ **dawn upon:** be revealed to
fearfully: terrifyingly

It was the story of a man who, in childhood, long ago, had chanced upon a book, in which there was a picture that frightened him. He had grown up and forgotten it and one night, upon a lonely railway platform, he had found himself in the remembered scene of the picture; he had confronted the solitary figure under the lamp; recognised it, and fled in panic. He had taken shelter in a wayside cottage; had been led to an upper room, found the book awaiting him and had begun to read it right through, to

10 *the very end, at last— And this book, too, was called* The Midnight Express. *And it was the story of a man who, in childhood—It would go on thus, forever and forever, and forever. There was no escape.*

But when the story came to the wayside cottage, for the third time, a deeper suspicion began to dawn upon him, slowly, fearfully, inevitably—Although there was no escape, he could at least try to grasp more clearly the details of the strange circle, the fearful wheel, in which he was moving.

20 There was nothing new about the details. They had been there all the time; but he had not grasped their significance. That was all. *The strange and dreadful being that had led him up the crooked stair—who and what was That?*

The story mentioned something that had escaped him. The strange host, who had given him shelter, was about his own height. Could it be that he also—and was this why the face was hidden?

At the very moment when he asked himself that

30 question, he heard the click of the key in the locked door.

The strange host was entering—moving towards him

chanced upon: found by chance, by accident
frightened him: terrified him, made him afraid

fled: ran away; flee, fled, fled □ **wayside:** situated at the side of the road □ **led:** conducted
right...end: completely to the end
at last: finally

go on thus: continue in this manner
forever: for ever, for always

third: first, second... □ **deeper:** more profound □ **dawn upon him:** come into his mind □ **although:** even if
at least try: make a minimal effort
wheel: turning circle

dreadful: terrible □ **being:** creature

that had escaped him: that he had not noticed
about: approximately
his own height: as tall as he was
hidden: unrevealed
very: exact

from behind—casting a grotesque shadow, larger than human, on the white walls in the guttering candlelight.

It was there, seated on the other side of the fire, facing him. With a horrible nonchalance, as a woman might prepare to remove a veil, it raised its hands to unwind the cerecloth from its face. He knew to whom it would belong. But would it be dead or living?

There was no way out but one. As Mortimer plunged forward and seized the tormentor by the throat, his own
10 throat was gripped with the same brutal force. The echoes of their strangled cry were indistinguishable; and when the last confused sounds died out together, the stillness of the room was so deep that you might have heard—the ticking of the old grandfather clock, and the long-drawn rhythmical "ah" of the sea, on a distant coast, thirty-eight years ago.

But Mortimer had escaped at last. Perhaps, after all he had caught the midnight express.

It was a battered old book, bound in red buck-
20 ram...

guttering: vacillating
seated: sitting

remove: take off □ **raised:** put up
unwind: unroll □ **to whom it would belong:** whose face it was

way out: solution □ **but:** except
throat: front of neck (= part of body joining head to trunk)
gripped: seized □ **the same:** similar
strangled: suffocated □ **indistinguishable:** impossible to distinguish □ **died out:** became inaudible □ **together:** simultaneously
might: could possibly

escaped: liberated himself □ **perhaps:** maybe
caught: taken

Grammaire au fil des nouvelles

En traduisant les phrases suivantes qui contiennent des difficultés grammaticales suggérées par les italiques, essayez de retrouver le texte anglais dont la page est indiquée par le premier chiffre et les lignes par les suivants ; les chiffres en gras renvoient à la Grammaire active *de l'anglais publiée au Livre de Poche.*

Tous les autres avaient *permis à la nuit d'entrer à flots* (112. 9-10).

Cela lui *donnait l'impression de vivre* intensément (112. 12. **p. 62**).

... à la *cinquantième* page qu'il ne pouvait *supporter de regarder* (112. 24. **pp. 86, 150**).

... comme il *se serait peut-être empressé de passer devant* un coin sombre (112. 28. **p. 26**).

Son attitude était tendue *comme s'il attendait quelque* catastrophe épouvantable (114. 12-13. **pp. 161, 36**).

Il *ne* pouvait *ni* résister à la fascination exercée par ce livre, *ni* affronter cette image (114. 16. **p. 163**).

Il *verrait* ce visage qui avait été dissimulé *si longtemps* (116. 10. **pp. 42, 154**).

Cela *devrait être* facile à faire pour un adulte (116. 14. **p. 24**).

Il vit *sans pouvoir parler* (116. 19-20. **pp. 148, 22**).

Il entendit *résonner* le bruit des pas (118. 9. **p. 60**).

S'il *pouvait* l'atteindre à temps, il *pourrait peut-être* y trouver de quoi s'abriter (118. 14. **p. 22**).

Il n'y avait pas d'autre lumière *excepté celle* du feu (120. 12).

L'hôte étrange entrait, projetant une ombre grotesque, *plus grande que nature* (122. 32 - 124. 2. **p. 114**).

Il savait *à qui il appartiendrait* (124. 6. **pp. 152, 42**).

Le silence de la chambre était *si profond que l'on aurait pu y entendre* le tic-tac de l'horloge franc-comtoise (124. 13-14. **pp. 164, 26**).

Vocabulary

— A —

above au-dessus de
abruptly brusquement
abstract résumé
accord (of its own —) de son plein gré
account for expliquer
ache faire mal
achieve réussir
acre demi-hectare (approx.)
act jouer (théâtre)
actually en réalité
acute aigu
adorn orner
afeard (dialect) effrayé
afraid (be — of) avoir peur de
after all après tout, en fin de compte
afternoon après-midi
against contre
agonize faire souffrir
ahead of devant
ajar entrebâillé
albeit quoique
alive en vie
all tout
all the same tout de même
all very well bien beau
alley passage
allow (for) permettre
alone seul
alone (leave —) tranquille
aloud à haute voix
already déjà
also aussi
although bien que, quoique
altogether complètement
among parmi
angle for chercher à obtenir indirectement

annoy agacer, irriter
answer réponse
anyhow de toute façon
anyway 1) de toute façon 2) à propos
apart à l'écart
apart from mis à part
apologise s'excuser
appal terrifier
appointment rendez-vous
armchair fauteuil
arouse éveiller, susciter
as 1) pendant que 2) puisque
ascertain s'assurer de
asleep (fall —) s'endormir
astonish étonner
attempt essai
attendant gardien
available disponible
avenging vengeur
avert détourner
avoid éviter
await attendre
awake éveillé
awake, awoke, awoken s'éveiller
awaken se réveiller
aware conscient
away absent
awful affreux, terrible

— B —

bachelor flat garçonnière
back-street petite rue
bad lot mauvais sujet
balance équilibre
balance sheet bilan
bandage pansement

bandage mettre un pansement sur
bang coup (violent)
banish bannir
barred strié
barrow stand (fruits et légumes)
base ignoble
basically en fait
bastard salaud
bat chauve-souris
bath cubes sels de bain
bathe bain de mer
battered tout abîmé
battle se frayer un chemin
bawl brailler
bay (keep at —) tenir à distance
beach plage
bear, bore, borne porter, supporter
bear away emporter
bear down on foncer sur
beast bête
beat, beat, beaten battre
beckon (sb. in) faire signe (à qqn d'entrer)
bedclothes draps et couvertures
before devant
begin, began, begun commencer
begrudge partager à contre-cœur
behalf (on — of) au nom de
behave se conduire (bien)
behind derrière
believe croire
bell cloche, sonnette
belong to appartenir à
below au-dessous de
below en bas
bend down, bent, bent (se) pencher, (se) baisser
beneath en bas
beneath sous

berth (give a wide —) éviter à tout prix
beside à côté de
besides en plus
bet parier
betray trahir
bewilderment désorientation
bewitch ensorceler
beyond au-delà de
bind, bound, bound (re)lier
bird oiseau
bishop évêque
bit partie
bit (a —) un peu
bite, bit, bitten ronger
blackmail chantage
blank vide
blanked-out effacé
blanket couverture
blaze brasier
bleed, bled, bled saigner
blend mélange
blind aveugle
blinded aveuglé
blood sang
bloody couvert de sang
blotting-paper (square of —) papier buvard (sous-main)
blow, blew, blown souffler
bluebottle mouche à viande
blurred flou
board planche
boast se vanter
boat bateau
body corps
booze boisson alcoolisée
bored (be —) s'ennuyer
borrow emprunter
bother (s')inquiéter, déranger
bottle (hit the —) lever le coude
bounce faire des bonds
bounder type

brace oneself se préparer mentalement
brain cerveau
brain assommer
brake frein
brandy cognac
brave courageux
break coupure, interruption
break, broke, broken (se) casser, (se) rompre
break down tomber en panne, s'effondrer
break into a run se mettre à courir
breath souffle
breath (out of —) essoufflé
breathless essouflé
bridal nuptial
bride mariée
bridge pont
briefcase serviette
bright brillant
brim over déborder
bring, brought, brought amener
bring up élever
broad large
broadcast, -cast, -cast diffuser
brocade brocart
brood upon méditer sur
broody préoccupé, songeur
brown brun
brush pinceau
bucket seau
buckram bougran, toile gommée
bug punaise
bulb ampoule
bunch bouquet
bundle ballot
burglar cambrioleur
burn, burnt/burned, burnt/burned brûler
burst éclat
burst, burst, burst éclater

bury enterrer
business-like efficace, sérieux
but sauf
buy, bought, bought acheter
by 1) près de 2) dès, avant

— C —

cab taxi, fiacre
cake of soap savonnette
candle bougie
candlestick bougeoir
candyfloss barbe à papa
canvas toile
caper numéro
care soin
care about s'intéresser à
care to do avoir envie de faire
cart charrette
carve tailler
cast, cast, cast (pro)jeter
castle château
catch, caught, caught attraper
cautiously prudemment
cave grotte
ceiling plafond
cerecloth linceul, toile d'embaumement
chain enchaîner
chalk craie
chance upon trouver par hasard
chap (little —) type (petit bonhomme)
charcoal fusain
charwoman femme de ménage
chat tête-à-tête
chatter 1) jacasser 2) claquer (dents)
cheek joue
cheerfully gaiement

cheerfulness bonne humeur
cheerily joyeusement
chest poitrine
chief(ly) principal(ement)
childhood enfance
chill refroidir
chilly froid
chime carillon
chin menton
choke étrangler
christening baptême
Christmas-eve Saint-Sylvestre
chuck abandonner
church église
circle faire le tour de
clang retentir
clang shut se refermer bruyamment
clap applaudir
clasp étreindre
clatter cliquetis
clattering bruyant
clear dégagé, tranquille (conscience)
clench serrer
clever habile
climb grimper
clip together attacher
cloak cape
clock (grandfather —) horloge (franc-comtoise)
cloister cloître
close 1) près 2) lourd
close (se) fermer
clothes vêtements
clutch accès
clutch serrer fort, se cramponner à
coach carrosse
coal charbon
coast côte
coat manteau
coating couche
coax cajoler
cobble pavé rond
cockerel jeune coq

coffin cercueil
coir-carpeted recouvert de moquette en noix de coco
cold rhume
collar col
come to oneself, came, come revenir à soi
come upon/across rencontrer
comfortingly de manière réconfortante
common sense bon sens
commonplace banal
companionable sympathique, chaleureux
conceal dissimuler
convey exprimer
cool frais
copy texte publicitaire
copywriter rédacteur publicitaire
corner coin, angle, recoin
coster marchand des quatre saisons
cough tousser
countryside paysage
course (of —) bien sûr
courtship (their —) l'époque où il lui faisait la cour
coward lâche
cram on the brakes freiner à mort
crash fracasser
crave désirer ardemment
craving désir ardent
crawl ramper
creak grincer, craquer
creep, crept, crept se glisser
creeps (give sb. the —) donner la chair de poule à qqn
crisp frais
crooked tournant (escalier)
cross traverser
cross oneself se signer

crossroads carrefour

crow (cock- —) chant du coq

crowd foule

crown sommet

crumb miette

crumble s'effriter

cry 1) s'écrier 2) pleurer

cultured cultivé

currant jelly gelée de groseilles

curse malédiction

cut off isolé

cut teeth, cut, cut faire ses dents

— D —

damn (God — it!) nom de Dieu !

damn (not give a — about) se ficher éperdument de

dare oser

daring audace

dark sombre

dark (after —) après la tombée de la nuit

dark(ness) obscurité

darken assombrir

dash se précipiter

daughter fille

dawn aube

dawn upon sb. venir à l'esprit de qqn

day-dreaming songeur

dead mort

deaf sourd

deal (a great/good — (of)) beaucoup (de)

dear cher

death mort

decade décennie

decent digne du nom

deceptive trompeur

definite net

degree licence

delayed à retardement

deliberation précaution

dent bosselure

deny sb. sth. priver qqn de qqch

depend upon compter sur

desk bureau (meuble)

desolate désert

determine décider

deuce (the — of a...) un sacré...

device dispositif

devoutly sincèrement

dew rosée

die mourir

die away, out s'éteindre (bruit)

dig, dug, dug enfoncer

dim terne, sombre

dip creux, déclivité

direct ordonner

directions instructions

directorial (— policy) politique imposée par la direction

dirty sale

disbelief incrédulité

discard rejeter

discontent mécontentement

disorder déranger

dispassionately avec détachement

dispel dissiper

dispute contester

distressed affligé

disturbance bruit

disturbing inquiétant

dividers compas

do sb., did, done faire sa fête à qqn

dodge esquiver, se faufiler

doodle griffonner distraitement

doomed condamné (à mourir)
door porte
doorway porche
double bed grand lit
downstairs en bas
drama théâtre
draught courant d'air
draughty plein de courants d'air
draw, drew, drawn (at)tirer
draw near approcher
draw on puiser dans
draw up se ranger (voiture)
drawer tiroir
drawing dessin
dread angoisse
dreadful affreux, terrible
dream rêve(r)
dreary lugubre
dress robe
dress up se déguiser
dressed in vêtu de
drill marteau-piqueur
drily sèchement
drink, drank, drunk boire
drip bruit de l'eau qui goutte
drive allée privée
drive, drove, driven 1) conduire 2) pousser
drooping penché
drop laisser tomber
drowsy assoupi
drunk ivre
dry sec
dry sécher
dual controls double commande
dull sans intérêt
dumb muet
dusk crépuscule
dust poussière
dustbin poubelle
dwarf nain

dwell upon, dwelled/dwelt, dwelled/dwelt s'étendre sur

— E —

eagerly ardemment, avec empressement
ear oreille
early tôt
earnestly avec sérieux
earth (what on —) que diable
earthly de ce monde
easy-chair fauteuil
eat, ate, eaten manger
echo se répercuter
edge se faufiler
edge (re)bord, chant
edge (on —) à vif
egg œuf
elbow coude
elder aîné
else autre
embrace étreinte, enlacement
empty vide, désert
encounter rencontrer
encroach envahir
end bout, fin
end (se) terminer; mettre fin à
endowed with doté de
engine moteur
enjoy aimer
entertain recevoir
escape délivrance
even même
evening soir
ever (where —?) où diable?
evidence témoignage
exchange central (téléphone)
exclaim s'écrier
exhaustion épuisement

exhibit exposer
expect s'attendre à, attendre
expectant attention attente
explanation explication
extension poste (téléphone)
extra supplémentaire
extravagance prodigalité
exultantly de manière triomphante
eye (keep an — on sb.) surveiller qqn

— F —

face affronter
factory usine
fade (away) s'affaiblir
fail ne pas fonctionner
faint faible (son)
faint (be in a —) s'évanouir
fairly assez
fairytale conte de fées
fall, fell, fallen tomber
fancy élaboré, beau (ironique)
far éloigné
faraway lointain
fathom comprendre
fear peur
fearful effroyable
feature mettre en vedette
feel, felt, felt sentir
felt-tip stylo-feutre
fetch aller chercher
feverish fiévreux
field champ
fiend démon
fierce 1) féroce 2) intense
fierily (to explode —) s'embraser
fight, fought, fought se battre
figure 1) silhouette 2) personnage

filing cabinet classeur (meuble)
find, found, found trouver
find out se renseigner
fine 1) beau 2) brave
finger doigt
fire feu
fire-escape escalier de secours
fireman pompier
fireplace cheminée
fist poing
fit crise
fit back réintégrer
fitful agité
flap (s')agiter
flare s'embraser
flash lancer des éclairs
flash (in a —) tout d'un coup
flask flacon
flee, fled, fled (s'en)fuir
flesh chair
flicker vaciller
flight vol
flight (of stairs) escalier
fling, flung, flung jeter
fling up ouvrir brusquement
flood inonder
flood flot, inondation
flood in entrer à flots
floor 1) sol, plancher
2) étage
floozie pouffiasse
flow together se confondre
flurry rafale
flush rougir
flutter s'agiter
fly mouche
fly open (flew, flown) s'ouvrir brusquement
fly out s'envoler
foggy (with smoke) enfumé
fold plier
follow suivre

fond (be — of) avoir de l'affection pour

fool imbécile

fool about traîner, perdre son temps

foot pied

footman valet de pied

footstep (bruit de) pas

for car

forbidding menaçant

forehead front

foretaste avant-goût

forewarned is forearmed un homme averti en vaut deux

forget, forgot, forgotten oublier

forgiveness pardon

formally sur un ton officiel

fortitude courage

four-poster bed lit à baldaquin

fragrant parfumé

frame encadrement

freeze, froze, frozen geler

friendless inhospitalier

fright effroi

frighten effrayer

frosty glacial

fudge fondant

fully complètement

fun amusement

funk sb. se dégonfler devant qqn

funny drôle

furnace-pipe tuyau de chaudière

fuss petits soins

fuss (make, kick up a —) faire des histoires, faire un esclandre

— G —

game jeu ; partie

gamut gamme

gasp halètement

gasp haleter, avoir le souffle coupé

gather s'assembler

gauge jauge

gaunt lugubre

gaze contempler

geld châtrer, hongrer

genial sympathique

gently doucement

get (+ adj.), got, got devenir

get away s'échapper

get away with en être quitte pour

get on progresser

get out of the way of + ing perdre l'habitude de

get rid of sth. se débarrasser de qqch

get up se lever

ghastly livide, spectral

ghost fantôme

ghostly spectral

gibber bégayer

gift don

girl fille

give (oneself) up, gave, given renoncer ; (se) rendre

give away trahir

give back reculer

give out s'épuiser

glad content, ravi

glance (cast a —) jeter un coup d'œil

glare éclat aveuglant

glimmer luire

glisten scintiller

gloom obscurité

glow 1) rougeoyer 2) rayonner, brûler

go (+ colour), went, gone devenir

go on (+ ing) continuer (à faire)

go out s'éteindre

go over passer en revue

goat chèvre

gold or

gold (as good as —) sage comme une image

good-looking séduisant

gossamer fils de la Vierge (nom); très fin (adj.)

graceful gracieux

grape raisin

grasp saisir

grass herbe

grate âtre

grave tombe

greatly grandement, fort

greet saluer

greeting salutation

greyish-haired aux cheveux grisonnants

grief douleur, chagrin

grieve pleurer (un mort)

grip saisir

grove (olive —) oliveraie

grow (up), grew, grown s'accroître (grandir, devenir adulte)

growl grogner

gruesome épouvantable

guest invité

guidance conseils

gust souffle

gutter 1) dégouliner (cire) 2) vaciller (flamme)

— H —

hacket entaille

hail héler

hall entrée

halt sign (ignore a —) brûler un stop

hammer marteau

hand main

hand (near at —) tout près

handbag sac à main

handsome beau

handy (come in —) être utile, pratique

hang on to sth. ne pas lâcher qqch

hang round sb. tourner autour de qqn

hang sb. (hanged, hanged) pendre qqn

hang, hung, hung 1) suspendre 2) pendre, planer

happen arriver

happen to do se trouver à faire (par hasard)

happiness bonheur

hard énergiquement

hardly à peine

harm (du) mal

hastily à la hâte

hat-pegs portemanteau

hate haine

hatred haine

haze vapeur

hazy (be — about) ne pas bien se rappeler

head tête

head off écarter, désamorcer

headache mal de tête

headed intitulé

healthy en bonne santé

hear, heard, heard entendre

heart cœur

hearth foyer

heartless sans cœur

heaven ciel, paradis

heavenly divin

heavy lourd

heed prêter attention à

heel talon

height hauteur

hell enfer

hell (where the —) où diable

help oneself se servir
herd out évacuer en troupeau
hide, hid, hidden/hid (se) cacher
high haut
hilly accidenté
hint indice
hit, hit, hit frapper
hold, held, held tenir, contenir
hold out tendre
hold up retenir, retarder
hollow creux
holy saint
home-bound qui ramène à la maison
hoot klaxonner
hope (for) espérer
horrid affreux, hideux
host hôte
hot chaud
house-party partie de campagne
housekeeper gouvernante
housemaid bonne
however cependant
huge immense
hum fredonner
hunched rentré
hung with orné de
hungry (be —) avoir faim
hurl oneself se jeter
hurry se précipiter
hurt, hurt, hurt blesser
husband mari
hush calme
hush! taisez-vous !
husky rauque
hustle se bousculer

— I —

ice glace
ice-cream glace
icicle glaçon
ill malade
ill-intention malveillance
illness maladie
impassioned plein de passion
impressive impressionnant
in print en caractères d'imprimerie
inch pouce (2,5 cm)
inch-thick épais d'un ou de plusieurs pouces
including y compris
increasingly de plus en plus
indeed en effet
inefficient inefficace
ink encre
instance (for —) par exemple
instead (of) au contraire, (au lieu de)
instructor moniteur
intercom interphone
intrude faire intrusion
involve impliquer
iron fer

— J —

jarr on sb. irriter, agacer qqn
johnny-know-all monsieur je-sais-tout
joke rigoler
jolt back ramener brutalement
jump sauter
jump up se lever d'un bond
junction gare de jonction

— K —

keen enthousiaste
keen (be — on + ing) se passionner pour
keep (away from), kept, kept garder, tenir (à l'écart de)
keep + ing continuer à faire
keep sb. + ing (waiting) forcer qqn à faire (faire attendre)
keep still rester tranquille
keep to se limiter à
key clef
kick (out) donner des coups de pieds, cogner
kid gosse
kill tuer
kind sorte
kind gentil
kindly plein de bonté
kindly (+ verb) vous êtes prié de
kiss embrasser
kiss baiser
knee genou
knife couteau
knighted (to be —) être fait chevalier
knock frapper, cogner
knock down, over renverser
knocker heurtoir
knot nouer
know, knew, known savoir
knuckle articulation (doigt)

— L —

lace dentelle
lack manquer de
landmark point de repère
large grand
largely en grand nombre
lash cil
last durer (longtemps)
latch loquet
lately ces derniers jours, récemment
latter dernier
laugh rire
laugh at se moquer de
laughter rires
laundry blanchisserie
lawn pelouse
lay down, laid, laid poser
layer couche
layout mise en page
lead, led, led diriger, conduire
leaf, leaves feuille
lean, leant/leaned, leant/leaned s'appuyer
leap saut
leap, leapt/leaped, leapt/leaped sauter
leash (let sb. off the —) lâcher la bride à qqn
least (at (the) —) au moins
leave out exclure
leave, left, left laisser, quitter
left (-hand) gauche
leg jambe
lemming lemming
lend, lent, lent prêter
length longueur
let, let, let louer (mettre en location)
let out disculper
library bibliothèque
lie (down), lay, lain être couché, (se coucher)
lie about traîner
life and soul (the — of the party) boute-en-train
lift ascenseur
lift (give sb. a —) prendre qqn en voiture

light lumière
light up prendre (feu)
light, lit/lighted, lit/lighted allumer, éclairer
lighting éclairage
lightly légèrement
lightning foudre
likely vraisemblable
limb membre
limb (young —) petit diable
linen linge
liner paquebot
linger persister
link lien
lip lèvre
lipstick rouge à lèvres
listen écouter
loathe détester
lock fermer à clé
log bûche
loneliness solitude
lonely seul, isolé
long-drawn soutenu
long-lost ancestral
look (take a — at) examiner
look avoir l'air, sembler
look away détourner son regard
look forward to attendre avec impatience
look here! écoutez !
look like ressembler
look over parcourir, feuilleter
look sb. up passer voir qqn
loose (shake oneself —) se détacher, se libérer
lord! mon dieu !
lore connaissances
lorry camion
lose, lost, lost perdre
loss perte
loud fort
lovely mignon
lower inférieur
luck chance

lucky (be —) avoir de la chance
lurch tituber, pencher

— M —

madman fou
maid servante
main door porte d'entrée
make (on the —) rapace
make + adj., made, made rendre
make for se diriger vers
make-up maquillage
malice malveillance
malignantly de manière malfaisante
manservant valet
manslaughter homicide involontaire
marble marbre
matter question, problème
matter (as a — of fact) en fait
matter (what's the —?) qu'y a-t-il ?
maudlin larmoyant
mean, meant, meant 1) vouloir dire 2) avoir l'intention de
means (by no —) nullement
meet, met, met rencontrer
melt se dissiper
mend arranger
mere(ly) simple(ment)
middle age (of —) = middle-aged d'un certain âge, entre deux âges
midnight minuit
might force
mile 1,609 kilomètres
mind esprit
mind avoir qqch contre

mind (have a good — to do) avoir bien envie de faire
mind you je vous assure
minute infime
miss manquer
mist brume
mistake erreur
moan gémir
mock simulé, feint
modest pudique
month mois
moonbeam rayon de lune
moonlight clair de lune
moor lande
moth papillon nocturne
motionless immobile
motor automobile
motor se déplacer en voiture
mourning deuil
move (over) bouger, se déplacer
move away s'éloigner
mud boue
multitudinous multiple
mumble marmonner
murder assassiner
mutter marmonner

— N —

nag harceler
nail ongle
nail, (— -studded) clou, (cloué)
nap somme
near s'approcher
near près (de), proche (de)
nearly presque
neck cou
neck (back of —) nuque
nerve nerf
never mind tant pis
nevertheless néanmoins
new nouveau

newsagent marchand de journaux
next à côté de
nightmare cauchemar
nightmarish cauchemardesque
nip goutte
nod faire un signe de tête
nod signe de tête
noise bruit
notice apercevoir
notice (take — of) prêter attention à
nought zéro
novel(ist) roman(cier)
nowadays de nos jours

— O —

oak chêne
oak-panelled lambrissé de chêne
oat crisps flocons d'avoine
obviously manifestement
occur to sb. venir à l'esprit de qqn
odd étrange
old vieux
once (all at —) tout d'un coup
openwork à claire-voie
otherwise sinon
out (have it — with sb.) s'expliquer avec qqn
outdistance semer, distancer
outer extérieur
outline contour
over plus de
overtop surplomber
overtake, -took, -taken rattraper
overwhelming écrasant
owe devoir
own propre

own (get one's — back) se venger
owner propriétaire

— P —

pace arpenter
pain douleur
palm paume
panelling boiseries
paper journal
part from quitter
particular difficile
past au-delà de
pat tapoter
path (way) chemin
patter tapoter
pavement trottoir
peace paix
peasant paysan
peg (take sb. down a —) rabattre le caquet à qqn
penny sou
performance représentation
pester harceler
petrol essence
pick one's way avancer avec précaution
pick up (re)prendre
picture tableau
picture-hat capeline
pier pile (d'un pont)
pile entasser
pillow oreiller
pin épingle(r)
pinch pincer
pine away languir, dépérir
pit trou profond
plainly clairement
plane-tree platane
play pièce (de théâtre)
playwright dramaturge
please yourself! comme vous voulez !

plenty of suffisamment de
plug in brancher
pocket-knife canif
point idée
point (there's no — in + ing) inutile de
point (to sth.) indiquer (qqch) du doigt
policy politique
poplar peuplier
post-war d'après-guerre
pouch blague (à tabac)
pound cogner
powder poudre
powerful puissant
praise éloge(s)
pram landau
premises locaux
preposterous absurde
presently peu après
pretend dissimuler, faire semblant
pretty assez
prevent empêcher
previous précédent
primrose (evening —) onagre, herbe aux ânes
prize (adj.) parfait
probe tâter
promising prometteur
prompt encourager
properly correctement
propose to sb. demander qqn en mariage
propped up bien calé
proud fier
provide sb. with sth. offrir, fournir qqch à qqn
pucker plissement
pull tirer
pull attrait, influence
pull oneself together se ressaisir
pull out sortir
purchase achat
put away, put, put ranger

put on side prendre des airs supérieurs
put oneself out se mettre en frais
put right arranger

— Q —

queer bizarre
quicken one's pace presser le pas
quiet calme, silencieux
quite tout à fait

— R —

rabbit lapin
race 1) courir 2) porter à toute vitesse
radiantly joyeusement
rags lambeaux
rail rampe
railway platform quai de gare
rambling vaste
random (at —) au hasard
range varier
rank rang
rap frapper
rap out débiter
rate (at any —) en tout cas
rather plutôt
rattle remuer bruyamment
rave délirer
reach atteindre
reach portée
read (right) through, read, read lire en entier
reassert oneself s'imposer à nouveau
recede reculer

receiver (replace the —) raccrocher
recognise reconnaître
recognition reconnaissance
recollection souvenir
recover oneself se ressaisir
reddish roussâtre
refill recharge
refrain (from + ing) se retenir (de faire)
regular vrai, véritable
relation parent
reluctant peu disposé
remain rester
remark faire observer
remember se souvenir de
remind (sb. of sth.) rappeler (qqch à qqn)
remote lointain, éloigné
remoteness isolement
remove enlever
rent louer (locataire)
reply réponse
reply répondre
repress réprimer
reproof désapprobation
required nécessaire
response réaction
rest repos
rest se reposer
rest (God — her soul) que Dieu ait son âme
restless agité
retort rétorquer
reverberate se répercuter
revulsion réaction, revirement
rib côte
rich (that's —!) c'est le comble !
ride voyage à cheval
riffle égrener rapidement
right directement
right bon, juste
right behind juste derrière
right up to tout près de

rights (put to —) arranger
ring cercle
ring, rang, rung sonner
ring out retentir
ring up appeler au téléphone
ripcord poignée d'ouverture
rise (up), rose, risen se lever
road route
roadway chaussée
roar hurler, mugir (vent), gronder (feu)
roll off débiter
romp gambader
roost se percher pour dormir
root racine
row boucan
rub frotter
rubbish des bêtises
ruddy rougeoyant
rude grossier
ruffle ébouriffer
ruffle manchette
rule règlement
rule (as a —) en général, en principe
run away s'écouler
run, ran, run tourner (moteur)
rush (se) précipiter
rustle bruissement
rustling bruissement, froissement

— S —

sad triste
saddle selle
safety sécurité
salesman représentant
sand sable
savagely furieusement
save + ing éviter de
saying expression

scarcely à peine
scared effrayé
scarlet écarlate
scatter éparpiller
scented parfumé
scowl se renfrogner
scratch gratter, rayer
scrawl griffonner
scream hurlement
scream hurler
screech crisser (pneu)
screech of laughter rire perçant
screen paravent
scrutiny examen
sea mer
search (in — of) à la recherche de
seat oneself prendre place, s'asseoir
see, saw, seen voir
seek, sought, sought chercher
send for, sent, sent faire venir
sensitive sensible
set, set, set préparer
set down noter
set sb. off about lancer qqn sur (sujet)
setting décor
settle régler
several plusieurs
shadow ombre
shake one's head dire non de la tête
shake, shook, shaken trembler
shame honte
shame (a —) dommage
share partager
sharp vif, pénétrant (esprit)
shed, shed, shed perdre (feuilles)
sheet drap
shelf étagère

shell coquillage
shelter abri
shelter (take) s'abriter
shift se remuer
shimmer chatoiement
shine, shone, shone briller
shiver grelotter
shoe chaussure
shoot, shot, shot foncer
shoot the works lâcher le
   morceau
shoot up s'ouvrir brusquement (fenêtre)
shorten raccourcir
shot coup (de pistolet)
shoulder épaule
shoulder-blade omoplate
shout crier
shout cri
shove poussée
show, showed, shown mon-
   trer
show sb. into a room faire
   entrer qqn dans une
   pièce
shower pluie
shriek hurler
shriek hurlement
shudder frisson(ner)
shuffle about gigoter
shuffling froissement
shut, shut, shut fermer
shut up enfermé
shut up se taire
sibilant sifflante
sickly maladif
sigh soupirer
sight (chose) vue
signpost poteau indicateur
silly 1) bête 2) dans un état
   second
silly (knock down —) faire
   perdre connaissance
silver argent
sink, sank, sunk descendre,
   s'enfoncer

sink (voice) se faire plus
   basse
sit, sat, sat 1) être assis 2)
   poser
sit down s'asseoir
sit up se redresser
site (building —) chantier
sitting séance
size taille
skating patinage
slam claquer
slam (into) enfoncer violem-
   ment
slash taillader
sleek brillant
sleep sommeil
sleep, slept, slept dormir
sleepy somnolent
sleet neige fondue
sleeve manche (vêtement)
slender mince
slide, slid, slid se glisser
slightly légèrement
slip (give sb. the —) fausser
   compagnie à qqn
slip aside s'écarter
slip away s'écouler
slip on enfiler
slouch(ed) hat chapeau à
   larges bords
slow down ralentir
slowly lentement
smart malin
smell odeur
smile sourire
smite, smote, smitten tour-
   menter (conscience)
smoke fumer
smoky brumeux
smooch bécoter
smooth lisser
smudge tache
snicket entaille
snowy neigeux
snuff moucher
soap savon

sob sangloter
sodden trempé
soft doux
soften s'adoucir
sole plante
solve résoudre
somehow d'une manière ou d'une autre
somewhat quelque peu
sooner or later tôt ou tard
soothe calmer
sooty noir de suie
sorry (make sb. —) faire regretter à qqn
soul âme
sound sembler (à entendre)
sound son
soundlessness silence
sovereign-case porte-monnaie
sparkle étinceler
spattered éclaboussé de boue
speak, spoke, spoken parler
speak well of dire du bien de
speechless muet
speed vitesse
spellbound subjugué
spill, spilt/spilled, spilt/spilled renverser
spineless mou, sans caractère
spirit esprit
spirit away enlever comme par enchantement
spite (in — of) malgré
spoil, spoilt/spoiled, spoilt/spoiled gâcher
spook fantôme
spoon cuillère
spoon out servir avec une cuillère
spot endroit
sprayed étalé comme une gerbe

square carré
squeeze écraser
staccato-voiced à la voix saccadée
staff personnel
stage 1) stade, étape 2) scène (théâtre)
stain tache(r)
stair(s) escalier
stallion étalon
stamp trépigner, taper du pied
stand, stood, stood 1) se tenir, rester debout 2) supporter
star vedette
stare fixer des yeux
start sursaut
start (down) commencer (à descendre)
start (up) sursauter, tressaillir
state état
stay away ne pas venir
steadily régulièrement
steal, stole, stolen voler
steam fumer
step faire un pas
stick, stuck, stuck 1) coller, coincer 2) supporter
stiff rigide, dur
still toutefois
still tranquille, silencieux
stillness silence
stink (to heaven) of sth., stank, stunk empester qqch
stippled pointillé
stir remuer
stirring enlevé
stirrup étrier
stomach ventre, estomac
stone pierre
stop (dead, short) s'arrêter (net)
storey étage

storm tempête
stove poêle
straight droit
straighten remonter (drap)
stranger inconnu
strap sangle
stream out flotter au vent
strenuous ardu
stretch (out) étendre
stride (take in one's —)
    accepter avec flegme
strike, struck, struck 1) frap-
    per, se heurter contre
    2) sonner
string fil, ficelle
striped rayé
strong fort
stuck in bed cloué au lit
study bureau (chez soi)
stumble trébucher
stump souche
stutter bégayer
suchlike semblable
suggestiveness puissance
    évocatrice
suit aller, convenir
sullen (-headed) renfrogné
sultry lourd
summon appeler
summon up rassembler
summons appel
sunny ensoleillé
surrender s'abandonner
surrounding environnant
swallow avaler, engloutir
swank esbroufe
swear, swore, sworn jurer
sweat transpirer
sweep, swept, swept 1) ba-
    layer 2) filer à toute
    allure
sweep away emporter
sweetheart mon amour
sweetness douceur
swell out, swelled, swel-
    led/swollen s'amplifier

swig lampée
swing open, swung, swung
    s'ouvrir brusquement
swing round se retourner
    rapidement
switchboard standard

— T —

tacky à moitié sèche (pein-
    ture)
take, took, taken emmener
take down noter
take in recevoir, héberger
take off enlever
take on engager
take out inviter
take place avoir lieu
take to sb. se prendre d'af-
    fection pour qqn
tale conte
tank up se soûler
tannoy interphone
tantalize tenter cruellement
tap tapoter
tap robinet
taper cierge
teach, taught, taught ensei-
    gner, apprendre
tear larme
tease taquin
tell, told, told dire, raconter
there voilà
there, there allons, allons
thick-set trapu
thickness épaisseur
thin mince, fin
thing (for one —, for ano-
    ther —) d'une part...
    d'autre part
think, thought, thought pen-
    ser
third troisième
third tiers

thoroughly complètement
though bien que
though (as —) comme si
thread fil, filet
threat menace
throat gorge
throng foule
throughout partout dans
throw (away), threw, thrown jeter (au rebut)
throw out étendre (bras)
thrust, thrust, thrust enfoncer, pousser, avancer brusquement
thus ainsi
ticking tic-tac
tidy bien rangé
tidy (up) ranger
tie lien
tighten (se) (res)serrer, (se) raidir
tiled carrelé
till jusqu'à ; jusqu'à ce que
time-switch minuterie
tingle vibrer
tinkle tintement
tinkle faire tinter
tiny minuscule
tiptoe marcher sur la pointe des pieds
tired (be — of + ing) en avoir assez de
tissue kleenex
tobacconist marchand de tabac
toe bout (chaussure)
tongue langue
tooth, teeth dent
tow remorquer
toward(s) vers
towel serviette (bain)
traffic circulation
trail traîner
tramp cargo, tramp
travel voyages
travel voyager

tray plateau
tread marche (escalier)
tree arbre
tremendous impressionnant
trick tour, farce
trouble ennui(s), inconvénient
trouble (get into —) s'attirer des ennuis
troublesome pénible
trump carte maîtresse, atout
trust avoir confiance (en)
truth vérité
try essayer
tub bac
tuck fourrer
tuck in border
tumble dégringolade
tumble dégringoler
turn (back, round) se retourner
turn away from (se) détourner
turn into s'engager (dans une rue)
turn sb. into transformer qqn
turn up se présenter, venir au rendez-vous
twig brindille
twilit crépusculaire
twist 1) tordre 2) zigzaguer
twisting tortueux
typewriter machine à écrire

— U —

umbrella parapluie
unbearable insupportable
unconvinced non convaincu
understand, -stood, -stood comprendre
undoubted indiscutable

undoubtedly incontestablement

undress se déshabiller

uneasiness malaise

uneasy mal à l'aise

unexpected inattendu

unfasten défaire

unfold déferler

ungracious impoli

uninhabited inhabité

unlock ouvrir

unmistakably incontestablement

unpleasant désagréable

unshaven non rasé

unutterably d'une manière indescriptible

unwind, unwound, unwound dérouler

up (be —) être levé

upper supérieur

upset bouleversé

upstairs en haut

upwards vers le haut

used (be — to + ing) être habitué à

used (get — to + ing) s'habituer à

useless inutile

usual (as —) comme d'habitude

utmost plus grand

utter exprimer, prononcer

utter(ly) total(ement)

— V —

vacuum cleaner aspirateur

van camionnette

vanish disparaître

vault 1) caveau 2) chambre forte

vault sauter

veil voile

vengeful vengeur

verge accotement

very (adj.) même

vicariously par personne interposée

virgin virginal

void vide, abîme

— W —

waft bouffée

wail gémir, se lamenter; hurler

wait attendre

wake, woke/waked, woken (up) (se) réveiller

waken (se) réveiller

waking éveillé

wall mur

wander about errer sans but

wander off s'éloigner tout seul

want (for — of) faute de

warm chaud, chaleureux

warn prévenir

warning avertissement

wash laver

washroom toilettes

waste désert

waste perdre (temps)

wastepaper basket corbeille à papiers

watch observer

watchful vigilant

watchman (night-) gardien (de nuit)

wave vague

wax cire

way in entrée

way out solution

wayside situé au bord de la route

wedge entaille

weep, wept, wept pleurer

well puits
welshman gallois
wet humide
wheel roue, cngrcnage
whereas tandis que
while espace de temps, bon moment
while pendant que
whimsical fantaisiste
whirlwind tornade
whisper chuchoter
whisper chuchotement
whistle siffler
whitewashed blanchi a la chaux
whole entier
why eh bien, ma foi
wick mèche
wide large
widower veuf
width largeur
will testament
willing prêt
willingly de bon cœur
willy-nilly bon gré mal gré
win, won, won gagner
wind vent
wind (put the — up sh.) flanquer la frousse à qqn
window fenêtre
windy venteux
wine vin
wing pile
wintry hivernal
wit(s) esprit, intelligence
witch sorciere

withdraw, -drew, -drawn (se) retirer
withered flétri
withering méprisant, désapprobateur
within 1) à l'intérieur de 2) en moins de
witness assister à
witty spirituel
wonder se demander, s'intertoger
wood bois
wooden en bois
word mot, parole
work œuvre
worse pire
worshipper admirateur
worst pire
worthy digne
wrap envelopper
wrapped up (in sth.) absorbé (par qqch.)
wreathed enveloppé
wreck loque
wrestle lutter
wriggle se tortiller

— Y —

yawn bâiller
yet pourtant
yet (not —) pas encore
yield céder
youngster jeune garcon

Achevé d'imprimer en mai 2012 en Espagne par
BLACK PRINT CPI IBERICA
Sant Andreu de la Barca (08740)
Dépôt légal 1ʳᵉ publication : mai 1992
Édition 07 – mai 2012
LIBRAIRIE GÉNÉRALE FRANÇAISE – 31, rue de Fleurus – 75278 Paris Cedex 06

30/8638/6